Amazon Advertising: A How-to Guide

Amazon Marketing Services Made Easy

by Lauren J. Gomez

For JG, GG, and LG.

Table of Contents

Introduction

The Amazon Marketing Services platform can be pretty amazing...*if* you know how to use it. I have been running very successful (and a few not-so-successful "learning opportunity") campaigns on AMS since the near inception of the platform. While I continue to be awestruck by the results, the platform is not always intuitive or easy to analyze. I have created hundreds of campaigns across the three AMS advertising types, and after lots of testing and analysis, I have come up with a set of best practices that have worked for me and the products I have helped to sell on Amazon. I am not formally affiliated with Amazon in any way, just an avid user of the platform with a lot to share. This book is for

Amazon sellers looking to start or improve these campaigns on their own.

As with most online businesses, nothing stays the same for long! The following chapters describe the AMS platform as it exists at the time of this writing. It will undoubtedly continue to evolve and improve. With so many vendors participating and providing feedback on the platform, expect continuous tweaks and updates in Amazon's interface, reporting and placement. However, the principles of advertising on Amazon will remain the same and this will allow me to guide you through the process, however the AMS platform may eventually end up looking.

You can find a wealth of basic information about Amazon Marketing Services on the Amazon site or through your Amazon account rep (if you are a big enough vendor to have an account rep, although most do not). But most everything I found was one-sided, all put out by Amazon. Helpful, yes—but definitely not the entire picture. I want to share my experiences with AMS from a vendor's perspective so that others can have an inside look at advertising on Amazon. Here is what I have learned!

Glossary of Terms

AAP: Amazon Advertising Platform. Advertising platform to target Amazon shoppers on Amazon-owned sites outside of Amazon.com.

ACoS: Advertising Cost of Sales. Metric in the main Amazon dashboard, calculated 100 * (Ad spend / Sales). The higher the ACoS, the worse the ad is performing relative to spend. ACoS is not commonly used outside of the Amazon Marketing Services platform.

aCPC/CPC: Average cost per click. The average price you pay when someone clicks your ad.

AMS: Amazon Marketing Services.

ASIN: Amazon Standard Identification Number. A 10-character alphanumeric unique identifier given to vendors by Amazon.com identifying a specific product.

Auction Based Pricing Model: A pricing model for buying ads. The advertiser bids the most he/she would pay for an ad, and the seller (in this case, Amazon) gives the ad space to the advertiser with the winning bid. However, the winner only is charged $0.01 more than the next highest bidder.

Auto Targeting: Hands-off type of keyword targeting in Sponsored Product Ads where the Amazon algorithm is used to match keywords with ads; the keywords aren't chosen by the advertiser.

Bid+: Feature available in Sponsored Product Manual Targeted ads that allows you to let Amazon automatically increase your maximum CPC bid up to 50% in order to increase your chances of getting the top placement on the search results page.

Brand Campaign: A Headline Search or Sponsored Products Manual Targeted campaign in which all the keywords used are related specifically to the product's brand name.

Campaign Ineligible: When a product or campaign is paused because the product does not meet the margin threshold set by Amazon. This can also happen if the ratings for this product fall below a threshold set by Amazon. Also may be seen as "Product Ineligible" which means the same thing, but for a *product* that is part of a larger campaign. The campaign will continue, but that product will no longer be shown. If a campaign only contains one product and that product becomes ineligible, then that campaign will not run at all.

Conquesting: Placing an ad on a competitor's product page.

Competitor Campaign: A Headline Search or Sponsored Products Manual Targeted campaign in which all the keywords used are related to your competitor's product/brand.

CTR: Click through rate. Calculated by number of clicks an ad receives divided by the number of impressions an ad gets.

DPV: Detail Page Views. The view is counted when a shopper clicks on an ad and the product's detail page loads.

Exact Match: Match type within Headline Search Ads and Sponsored Product Manual Target ads. Keywords set with this match type only serve an ad when the exact same keyword is typed in, without any other words.

HSA: Headline Search Ads. One of the three types of Amazon Marketing Services ads. These are keyword-targeted ads that appear *above* the search results on an Amazon search results page.

Impressions: How many times an ad was displayed to a shopper

In-market: Shoppers who are actively looking for a particular product or service. Example: Lisa is remodeling her kitchen in a couple weeks and is *in market* for a new faucet.

Inventory: Number of opportunities for ad placement on a page.

Manual Targeting: Type of keyword targeting in Sponsored Products ads where the advertiser chooses the keywords.

Non Brand Campaign: A Headline Search or Sponsored Products Manual Targeted campaign in which all the keywords used are *not* brand-specific, but rather, are only generic terms that could apply to *any* product in your category.

Organic Search Results: Listings on search engine (in this case Amazon's) results pages that show due to relevance to the search terms. Organic search results are not paid.

PPC: Pay per click. These are ads in which the advertiser is not charged for the ad unless an ad is clicked by a consumer. All Amazon Marketing Services ads are currently sold only on a pay per click basis.

PDP: Product Detail Page.

Phrase Match: Match type within Headline Search Ads and Sponsored Product Manual Target ads. Keywords set with this match type serves an ad when the keyword (or the keyword plus other words) is typed.

Prospecting: Advertising that focuses on potential customers.

ROAS: Return on Ad Spend. Calculated as Sales divided by Ad Spend. Can be expressed as a percentage or a dollar amount.

Sales: Sales of product on Amazon.com.

SERP: Search engine results page

Sponsored Products: One of the three types of Amazon ads. Ads of specific products are targeted by keywords.

Chapter 1 – What is AMS?

The stats about the world's largest retailer are astounding: According to its annual report, Amazon.com generated over $100 billion in sales in 2015 (and was the world's fastest company to reach that $100 billion mark), and had more than 237 million active accounts! In addition to the millions of sales generated every day, Amazon has another very large revenue stream created by allowing its vendors to advertise on its website. This is the modern day retailer-requested, vendor-funded program that many manufacturers know so well. However, instead of crossing your fingers and hoping your products fly out the door, with *this* program, you open your laptop, pull out your credit card, and take control of the process yourself!

AMS is Amazon Marketing Services, a self-serve advertising platform. By using this platform, you can personally create ad campaigns, thus influencing shoppers on Amazon.com and driving traffic to the products that you sell on Amazon. Better yet, you can get in this program starting with just a few dollars. Want the very first spot on the Amazon search results page? No problem. That is a completely realistic goal using AMS. Want to promote a brand new product you just listed? Easy. You can drive thousands of views in a day via AMS. Want to put a picture of your product directly under the "Buy" box for your top competitor? That, too, is possible, through AMS.

The self-serve nature of the platform allows vendors big and small to jump right in and take the reins in deciding the quantity and quality of the ads. This is great because you don't have to wait on anyone to develop your ads, implement them, etc. Much like Google AdWords, you just jump in and create it yourself. On the other hand, the burden is on you to figure out the best way to structure your ads, how many ads you should launch, what they should target, how much you should spend, and so on. When I started using AMS, I did so much testing (let's be honest—"guessing") on how to effectively set up campaigns to maximize visibility to how the campaign is performing on a weekly, biweekly or monthly basis. I want to save you the trial-and-error trouble I went through, so I will share what I tested, what has worked for me, and what lessons I have learned along the way.

WHY AMS?

AMS is simply amazing. I have seen completely incredible return on ad spend (ROAS) using AMS. You can earn thousands of dollars in sales for just a few hundred dollars of ad spend. Of course, this all depends on your product and your product category, but I know this tool has the potential to completely change your business on Amazon. It is also very simple, once you know how to get set up & analyze.

Amazon does have some other advertising opportunities like running ads via its Amazon Media Group platform, but for this book, I am only going to speak about the advertising method I know best— *advertising on Amazon.com for the products you are selling on Amazon.com*; this advertising program is wholly in the Amazon ecosystem. I enjoy running campaigns on Amazon; the results are amazing and you can easily test ad campaigns of varying length, placement, and cost. This is a very straightforward and direct ad platform, with the exception of things like the 14-day sales attribution window and the reporting, which we'll get into later.

HOW DO YOU GET STARTED?

Checklist of things you need before you begin:

- Credit card
- List of your products (if you don't have an intimate knowledge)
- Net Invoice Price by item

That's it! With these things at hand, you can be up and running in minutes.

First, go to the AMS homepage. From there, you will be asked to create an account. You must choose whether you have a Vendor Central login, an Advantage Central login, a Vendor Express login, a Kindle Direct Publisher account or you want to request an invitation to represent a vendor (like a digital ad agency). If at this point you know you don't have any of these, back up and get in touch with whoever at your company manages the Amazon account. If that's not you, you should get this person involved and communicate tightly with them throughout the set-up process and campaign. If you know your company has one of these accounts, your

Amazon account manager can add you to the AMS account via email. This process is pretty quick.

Now that you are logged in, make sure your brand appears on the top left and you are ready to select the "New Campaign" box. You will then have three choices: Sponsored Products, Headline Search, and Product Display. To move any further, you must select one. I'll go into each type in depth in later chapters.

Taking full advantage of all Amazon Search Ads have to offer can get very complex (especially if you sell a lot of products on Amazon!), and you could end up creating hundreds of ads, so before you get overwhelmed, take a deep breath. I have sorted out the types of campaigns into Phase I, Phase II and Phase III. I recommend starting with Phase I, and letting those ads run at least a few weeks until you get a feeling for how they are performing and see the (hopefully abundant) sales coming through. You can spend a lot or a little in Phase I—it's up to you. Then, you can move on to the ads in Phase II, and once you get the hang of those you can move on to Phase III if you want to do even more. However, you can run Phase I ads for quite a while and see great success without complicating things by moving into Phase II ads. The same goes for moving onto Phase III. Even if you *do* move to Phase III, the ads are relatively easy to set up and execute as long as you have your campaign structure set up and have a good handle on how to organize your campaigns.

If you are someone who can't wait and are perhaps creating the ad live while reading this (go for it!), at least skim through the sections detailing the different phases first—as once you create an ad on Amazon, there are elements you can edit and elements you *cannot* edit, and once an ad is created it *cannot* be deleted. I will repeat this for emphasis. *AN AD CANNOT BE DELETED*! It can be paused or terminated, but it will stay in your account in your AMS dashboard. Forever. (At least for now it's forever—Amazon does change things up continuously.) If you don't mind a cluttered view of your campaigns, don't worry about it, but I know enough particular people who don't want old/junk/dead campaigns messing up their dashboard view of the live ones. Hang tight—you can jump in momentarily!

TO PAY FOR CLICKS OR NOT PAY FOR CLICKS?

Here's one question that may have been gnawing at you since you first heard about this program: Why am paying to get sales that I am currently getting for free? This is a totally valid question, and it needs to be answered before you make AMS a part of your marketing arsenal. First, this emphasizes a tenet of this book—the need for testing. Test. Test. *Test*. I know enough to know that I *don't* really know what is going to happen, especially when it comes to shopping habits of the American public. However, you should be wary of paying for what you are getting now for free.

Here's a simple test: Start a few campaigns and measure sales on those products in a comparable time period. Then, take a look at your sales and the cost of getting those sales. If you do not see a measurable lift (all other things being equal, like seasonality) then you *shouldn't* spend the money to advertise on Amazon. However, if you are not advertising on Amazon and your competitors are, you *need to* jump in. You might be lucky enough to be in a category where other players are late to the game. If this is the case, you should jump in today—because your competitors might wake up tomorrow.

Here's what you probably don't want to hear: this is the cost of doing business on Amazon. Just as you may pay retailers a rebate, this is a rebate on its own—but with a definite upside: *you* can actually control these dollars and how they work for you. It's not just an arbitrary percentage you are paying; it's a tangible tool you can control and use to move the needle for your business. So, take that money and let's knock it out of the park!

TYPES OF ADS

I'll do an in-depth walkthrough of the three types of ads offered by Amazon within the AMS platform in Chapters 3-5, but here's a brief overview. Each ad serves a unique propose and targets customers in a different part of the purchase funnel: Headline Search, Sponsored Products and Product Display. Depending on your business, you might want to use all three or just focus on one or two. Here's a quick summary and the pros and cons of each.

GENERAL PROS & CONS OF EACH AD TYPE

Headline Search

What it is: Ads that appear at the top of the Search Results Page and are served based on keywords the shopper uses.

Pros: Most viewable, no scrolling required for shoppers to see the ad, biggest audience, ability to craft a message/use creatively to get attention.

Cons: Longer time to set-up (compared to Sponsored Products), limited inventory, more competitive (and therefore, more expensive).

Sponsored Products

What it is: Ads that appear on the product page or below the search results based on keywords the shopper uses.

Pros: Extremely easy to set up, lots of inventory, doesn't look like an ad.

Cons: Not many levers to pull to change performance after ads start, not as noticeable as Headline Search Ads

Product Display

What it is: Ads that appear mainly on a product detail page and are targeted by interest (as in other websites outside of Amazon.com) or product (other products on Amazon.com).

Pros: Can be very specific and targeted, encourages discovery of new products directly by a potential customer.

Cons: Generally fewer impressions, worse conversion as compared to other campaign types.

THE INVESTMENT

17

One of the best things about AMS is that you can start with a very small investment--as little as a dollar a day for some campaigns. You can actually make an impactful change on your business for very little risk. This is why you owe it to your business to at least test some ads. There is no downside! Of course, some categories may have more expensive keywords than others, but generally, you can see results for very little spend.

When you login to the AMS platform, you will see the dashboard immediately. This is the central hub for all your campaigns and any you have ever created will be listed here. Here you can see your spend, sales and several other metrics that can help you get a snapshot of how your ads are performing. I'll take you through the AMS dashboard column by column in the next chapter. The two biggest takeaways regarding the challenges of the dashboard: 1) you need to "discount" the sales reported in the dashboard to reflect your price to Amazon, and 2) the reporting is cumulative, so you can't see sales for a specific time period. I'll show you how to look at results in order to combat these challenges.

Ok, let's jump in!

Chapter 2 – Decoding the Dashboard

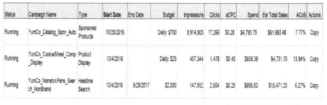

Status	Campaign Name	Type	Start Date	End Date	Budget	Impressions	Clicks	aCPC	Spend	Est Total Sales	ACoS	Actions
Running	YumCo_Catalog_Spon_Auto	Sponsored Products	10/25/2016		Daily: $700	9,914,905	17,266	$0.28	$4,790.75	$61,683.48	7.77%	Copy
Running	YumCo_CookieSheet_Comp_Display	Product Display	10/4/2016		Daily: $25	457,344	1,478	$0.45	$669.38	$4,731.70	13.94%	Copy
Running	YumCo_NonstickPans_Search_NonBrand	Headline Search	10/4/2016	5/29/2017	$2,000	147,562	2,654	$0.25	$656.83	$10,471.20	6.27%	Copy

Sample AMS Dashboard

KNOW YOUR NUMBERS

The Amazon Marketing Services dashboard is where
you see all the top-line information for ALL the
AMS ads. All ads—Headline Search, Sponsored
Products, and Product Display—are all shown
together on the dashboard, in the order you created
the ads (most recent first). So, it can be very difficult

to interpret the numbers when you are comparing ads of the *same type* that weren't created at the *same time*. The dashboard is shown on a historical basis—all spending, sales, impressions, etc. are cumulative from the time they are started. Since you will most likely not create all ads at the same time, it makes it impossible to really glean much weekly or monthly information from this view! You would expect a calendar select tool here to just show results from a certain time period. I'm sure this will become a feature at some point, but for now, you'll have to pull the results out of the reports to truly analyze the data. This is one reason why I created the Snapshots method. I'll go in depth in Chapter 6, but Snapshots is one way to capture the data week over week so you can easily compare the campaigns to each other and against your Return on Ad Spend (ROAS) targets.

> **TIP: You can easily sort every column, just by clicking the header. So you can sort it to show all the Headline Search Ads together at the top, or by most sales.**

So let's go through the columns at the top of the AMS dashboard. From left to right, these are the columns, they are the same for all campaign types and all can be found here:

Status: This shows the current status of the campaign: Terminated, Ended or Running. You can click here on a campaign that is running to change the status, pausing or terminating it. Note there is *not* a "delete" choice. Once you create a campaign, it is always there. Every campaign I have ever created still shows in the AMS dashboard *even* if it was terminated, ran out of budget, or ended based on the dates set for the campaign. Keep this in mind—the campaigns just pile up in the dashboard and never go away! Some people this doesn't bother, but if you are the type of person who really likes a clean inbox (for example), this will drive you nuts! Here are a couple of tips: Instead of creating new campaigns each time they expire, simply extend the end date rather than creating a new campaign if you don't want to change anything other than the end date. Also, think *very* carefully about your structure before naming the campaign, as we will discuss below.

Campaign Name: Do not take this column lightly because you cannot change it! Once you name your campaign and save it, there is no turning back. If you made a big mistake in naming it your only option is to terminate it and start again....but you can't delete a terminated campaign. I learned this lesson the hard way, and I am sharing it now so *you* don't have to! Just think through your naming convention before you start and if you do screw it up, know that it's not the end of the world (but certainly is a frustrating aspect of AMS, in my opinion)! I advise documenting your naming convention before you start and sharing it with anyone else who has access to the ad account and wants monitor the ads. I like to name the campaign first according to Product then CAMPAIGN TYPE, I do this in all caps because it's easier for me to see when looking through the dashboard. If you are selling men's leather band watches, you'd name a Search Campaign something like this: Men's Leather SEARCH NON-BRAND or this: MenLeather_Search_NonBrand. It's your preference here!

Type: This column shows the name of the type of campaign it is: Headline Search, Sponsored Products or Product Display. Like all columns, you can sort by clicking the header. That feature is particularly helpful here, because you can group like campaigns together, which helps a bit when editing. The default view shows the campaign by the most recently created first. It is helpful to sort the campaigns by type if you set up several of them and are going to analyze them by using the Snapshots Method.

Start Date: Date you started the campaign. All information in the dashboard starts at this date for each particular campaign. Let's say you have two campaigns in your AMS dashboard. You started the first one on September 1st. Then, you started your second campaign on November 15th. The dashboard information will be a culmination of all data from September 1st to present for Campaign 1 and from November 15th to present for Campaign 2.

End Date: The date a campaign ends. This can be in the past or the future. If you have a campaign that already ran and you either terminated it or it ran out of budget or ended, then that last date is shown. For other campaigns that are currently running, the end date shown is in the future if they have one or left blank if you chose the "Run Continuously" always-on option during set-up. You can run all three campaign types without an end date. You can select an end date, but since you can end them at any time, I leave mine running continuously. For Search campaigns, the campaigns do end on the end date but you can go in and move the end date after launch. You can change the end date at any time, so when you set it up initially, don't over analyze it; you can always go back and change it later if you desire.

Budget: This column shows the budget you chose for the campaign. The budget can be daily or for the campaign duration, depending on the campaign and what you select at setup. For Headline Search Ads or Product Display Ads, you can select budget caps for the day or for the entire campaign (you will choose the dates of the campaign). For Sponsored Product Ads, you can only select a daily budget and the minimum daily budget is $1. Great news if you are a small vendor just testing the waters!

For entire-campaign budgets, the minimum budget is $100, but this is for the duration. That doesn't mean you have to pay $100 immediately. If you choose $100 as your budget and make your campaign one month, you can distribute the spending over that month and spend less than $25 a week AND have the ability to pause or terminate at any time. So, if you are feeling iffy about starting out at $100 and don't want to risk it—you don't have to. You can test the waters in AMS for a lot less. You—of course—can add to the budget any time you want!

Impressions: Like other forms of digital advertising, impressions in the AMS platform means the number of times your ad was served and shoppers had the opportunity to see it. The longer a campaign is running, the more impressions that will build up in this column. If your campaign is not getting any impressions, your Cost Per Click bid is probably too low.

Clicks: This is number of times that someone clicked on your ad. At this point, you can calculate a click-through rate (CTR) if that is a metric you want to look at. If you are also running other pay per click ads, it would be a good idea to compare them against AMS ads and see where you are vs. Google, Facebook, Bing, etc. You calculate the CTR by dividing impressions by clicks. If you get 2,500,000 impressions and you get 800 clicks, then your CTR is 0.03%.

800 clicks/2,500,000 impressions

$= 0.00032 * 100$

$= 0.032\%$ CTR

CTR can vary widely depending on ad, product category, etc. but it is a common key performance indicator (KPI) for Search Ads that is *not* included in the AMS dashboard. If this is a KPI you want to track on a regular basis, then you can easily calculate it yourself in a spreadsheet created for analyzing sales week over week.

aCPC: This is the average cost per click. It is calculated by taking the entire campaign spend and dividing it by the number of clicks it received. The aCPC moves higher as competition in the category increases. Your aCPC will not necessarily match your max bid—it could be lower, as every ad you win may not be at your CPC max.

Spend: This is the amount of money you have spent on the campaign from when the campaign began. This view is cumulative only and doesn't show totals by any other time period (and that's why it's important to set up your Snapshots or another spreadsheet to a business intelligence system, as described in Chapter 6). Your spend is charged to the credit card that was entered when you set up your account. This spend number is specific to *that campaign only*. You cannot get total spend on all AMS campaigns without pulling the data into another sheet or system to analyze it.

Estimated Total Sales: Undoubtedly, the most important column, this column shows all of the sales that result from someone clicking an ad in that campaign. Sales data may take up to 3 days to show up in this column. Unfortunately, it's not as straightforward as it sounds. AMS uses a 14-day attribution window. This is very different from Google AdWords and many other pay per click (PPC) vendors. This means that if someone clicks on your ad, and doesn't purchase for a week, the ad that they saw gets credit for, or has the sales attributed, to the ad. Because of this, you could show spending but no sales for a week or two as the sales roll in. If you have other products under the same brand, those products get credit from the ad as well. This is where it can get tricky—after all, if you are working on additional efforts to increase Amazon sales, then you don't really know *what* is moving the needle. Was it the promo? Was it an e-blast driving your customers to Amazon? Retailers and brands everywhere are struggling with attribution, and there are lots of varying opinions on why, but the most important thing is to know what the window is and to take it in consideration with your other marketing programs.

ACoS: Advertising Cost of Sales. This metric is calculated by taking your spend and dividing it by your sales. The lower this percentage is, the better your ads are doing relative to spend. This is always calculated by spend from Day 1 of the campaign until today's date, and sales from the same period (which, remember, can take up to 14 days to be attributed and added to the total). So if you have an ACoS of 10%, then for every $1 in sales generated, you spent $0.10. Example: $1,000 spend/$10,000 sales

$$= 0.1 * 100$$
$$= 10\% \text{ ACoS}$$

I do not find this metric particularly helpful. I think at a quick glance it can be directionally helpful, but brands must think beyond this metric. Why? There is no margin component! You can't really analyze your campaigns or make any decisions without taking into account your net product sales.

Selling on Amazon isn't direct sales. You need to account for the cut you give Amazon. If you are using Google AdWords and drive customers to your website and spend $100 and get $1000 in sales directly from your brand's website, then your ACoS or Return on Ad Spend (ROAS) is 10%. If you spend $100 with AMS to drive $1000 of retail sales on Amazon the situation is a little different. If you sold Amazon your product for $500, your *true* ROAS is not $10, it would be $5.

> $1,000 retail sales - $500 company sales
> = $500 net sales / $100 cost of ads
> = $5 ROAS

ROAS is also expressed as a percentage, so it could also be 500%; I think it's easier to look at as a dollar amount.

Actions: I have only ever seen one type of action in this column, and it is "Copy." This is great, because initially this "action" didn't exist in AMS and copying is a huge advantage over creating campaigns from scratch each time. This is where you can copy an existing campaign to create a similar one quickly, allowing you to save some time on the basic set up (don't forget to change the campaign name!). You can copy any campaign—running, paused or terminated. This is great for when your campaign runs out and you forgot to extend it: you can just copy it and pick your new end date. The copy feature is also beneficial when you are testing creative in Search Ads or Display Ads: you simply copy the ad and the change the one element you want to test—for example, if you created a Display Ad and your

Headline message was "Charge your phone faster with the Acme Boost Charger" and you aren't getting a lot of clicks, you may decide to test the message "Durability and Speed: shop the Acme Boost Charger" to see how that does. To easily test the "durability" message, you simply "Copy" the first ad and flip out the Headline. You can now test just the change in the message. You can do the same with other elements of the campaign quickly by using the "Copy" feature, like if you have a Sponsored Products Campaign of only *branded* keywords, you could copy that campaign and clear out all the branded keywords and replace them with *non-branded* keywords.

You are up to speed on the dashboard. Let's fill it with sales now!

Chapter 3 – Headline Search Ads

As we covered earlier, 55% of shoppers start their search on Amazon above anywhere else, so Headline Search Ads are a way to make your product the very next thing they see after they click the search icon. Headline Search Ads are similar to the Google Search Ads we are all familiar with. The premise is similar: A shopper searches for a keyword like "watch" in the Amazon search bar. The advertiser bids in advance on keywords he thinks are related to his product: watch, timepiece, wristwatch, etc. The advertiser with the highest bid wins the placement and his ad for Tick-Tock Men's Premium Watches appears at the top of the search results.

Something great about the Amazon ads is that they are all contextual—meaning they are being served to shoppers who have the mindset of wanting to buy something. This is regardless of season or event-driven marketing. This may be a mind shift in your organization if you have a highly seasonal item. But with the scale of Amazon, it is not unusual to have shoppers looking for a pirate costume in April instead of October. With these ads, you can be ready to target those customers at *any* point in time!

Amazon Headline Search Ads appear above the search results on a results page, or SERP (search engine results page). Headline Search Ads appear based on keywords that the shopper types in the search like "multivitamins for men," "insulated coffee mugs" or "pneumatic nailer." Search Ads can sometimes look to shoppers like the first search *result*, not an ad—some customers click on them not even realizing they clicked on an ad. Using Search Ads is the way to ensure you get the **very first listing** on Amazon's SERP for a keyword, no matter what position Amazon's search algorithm ranks your product. For example, your product could be a solid page six item for the term "kids yellow raincoat" but you can flip that *in a day* by bidding the highest among other bidders for the term "kids yellow raincoat." As long as your product keeps converting from that keyword over time (Amazon can pause keywords in your campaigns at its discretion) and you have the winning bid (or only bid in some cases) that coveted top spot is yours to hang on to.

The top spot provides two benefits. First, you *did* snag that top spot (yay!) and shoppers are forced to scroll past your product to even see others products, perhaps providing exposure you would not have gotten otherwise. Second, this tactic *should* lead to more sales—and with more sales, over time your product will start to rise to the top of the SERP if you are outperforming the other results for this keyword. After a while, if all goes well, you could score the top search result *without* an ad.

Conversely, say you've been selling a children's yellow raincoat on Amazon for years, have the best-selling product and typically rank first for that search term. Then someone swoops in and buys the search term "kid's yellow raincoat" bumping you to down to the number two position. Yikes! That is the other side of the coin and the cold reality of Search Advertising (not just Amazon, but *all* search advertising). To get that #1 spot back, you may have to start bidding on and paying for a spot you previously earned for free. If that *does* happen, I will show you how to get that spot back and optimize your campaigns to maximize the money you do have to shell out.

Headline Search Ads can also be followed immediately by Sponsored Product Ads; I have seen this in highly competitive Amazon categories, like electronics. Sometimes there is a Search Ad followed by one or even two Sponsored Product Ads. Sponsored Product Ads can also appear on the SERP at the bottom, before you click to page two. So your Search Ad won't likely be the only ad on the page, but it *will be* in the top spot and it will look different—you will have a Headline after all. Unlike the Sponsored Product Ads that we just covered, the inventory for Headline Search Ads is a lot smaller: only the one listing per page. That's why these ads are competitive; there is just a single winner for high traffic search terms like "laptop." But just think—for all the laptops listed on Amazon, that ONE spot can be yours!

HOW TO GET STARTED

First, decide what type of campaign you are going to create. The order of the exact steps in the AMS tool may change as Amazon improves and upgrades the interface, but the first step will always be to decide what you are going to advertise and how to structure your campaigns! Deciding how/where to start is dependent on your product catalog within Amazon and your business. Unlike Sponsored Products that only show a single product at a time, these ads show up to three products based on a search term you bid on, and then lead to a landing page with several more of your products (not the Product Detail Page, as with Sponsored Product Ads). So, you can create broad campaigns (Headline: Gifts for your Valentine!) or narrow ones (Headline: Shop Toddler Yellow Raincoats), but decide what you want to tackle first before you go into the tool and start to actually create the ad.

To start, click on the "New Campaign" button on the top left of the AMS. You will then select the "Headline Search" ad option. Again, these ads are targeted by keywords and appear at the top of the SERP on Amazon, not on a Product Detail page. You will first curate a "landing page." Don't get deterred by this—it is very easy, and Amazon continues to make creating these ads more user-friendly. This is where shoppers will go if they click your ad—so think it through with that in mind: what got the customer there (a word(s) they typed in), what the customer clicked on (your product) and what the customer expects (that product for sure, and maybe some other related products of yours?)

TIP: Once you name a campaign, you cannot change it—so think carefully about your naming

> **convention. The default name will not give you info about what campaign it is, making it hard to analyze in the dashboard.**

CAMPAIGN STRUCTURE EXAMPLE

Campaign structure is as important in Search Ads as it is in Sponsored Products. It remains critical to keep Amazon Ads organized, allowing a proper analysis. Remember, all these new ads you are about to create are going to be in the same dashboard as your Sponsored Products campaigns, so organization and naming conventions continue to be important. Just as with Sponsored Products, you won't be running just one ad; you'll probably be running anywhere from a few to a few dozen. So, exactly how *should* you organize and name these ads? Let's walk through using an example business to illustrate options for campaign set-up as we go through the chapter.

Here's a fictional specialty bakeware company that sells to Amazon, Yum Co. Yum Co makes pans, cookie sheets, rolling pins, cake decorating supplies and cookie cutters. For Search Ads, Yum Co could create a campaign for each of those assortments. Yum Co can also create separate campaigns within the "pans" category for cake pans, brownie pans and non-stick pans. They can also create a campaign for the overall category of baking supplies. Each of these categories and campaigns will have its own keywords, and some will overlap each other. (Amazon ensures you will not compete against yourself.) You can see how it gets complicated! Be aware of potential saturation: for example, if there is not a ton of search volume in the "pans" category, you might be overdoing it to have three super-specific campaigns bidding on just a handful of generic keywords. We'll talk more in-depth on the campaign break-out and structure in the "Types of Search Campaigns" section later in this chapter.

THE LANDING PAGE

The landing page is a "curated" SERP or multi-ASIN page of your Amazon items you select that you want to sell. They should obviously include the item you showed in the ad as well as other related or similar products. Amazon has made this easier recently, so you can just click the products you want to add from your list and they will auto-generate below. You need to select at least three products; however, you can add several more—as many as you want. You need to know what you are advertising in order to plan your landing page at this point, so don't start adding products until you have your strategy firmly in place.

You want to think about how you select these products, as you cannot change them once the campaign is launched. If you start a campaign and realize you forgot to add a product, it's not a big deal. You can just copy your campaign, then re-do the landing page and terminate the original one. However, the campaign you started will stay on your dashboard. This is more annoying than hurtful, and it won't affect your ads!

If you only have less than 5-6 products on Amazon, you could just select them all. If you have more, think about the keywords that are in your campaign that are driving people there. If you have a few versions of an item, then make sure it is easy to tell the difference among them, as the last thing you want to do is pay to send a customer to your curated page and then confuse them! If you are listing similar products, you may want to add one product to your curated page and then other related, but dissimilar, products. You could set up the same campaign and list variations on the main product advertised and see which performs better. You never know until you test!

Once you start adding your products, they will show in the order you select them. Remember this: You may have to scroll up and down to get your products. Also, if you have resellers who also sell your products, they may get in that list. To be absolutely certain that you select the right product to advertise, you might want to just enter each ASIN in the order you want it to appear and then click "search," then add. Amazon allows you to preview what this page looks like when you are setting up your ad. Look in the "Campaign Summary" box to find this option. Definitely take a look and see how your page will appear to shoppers.

The alternative to a curated landing page is to send shoppers to your Amazon brand page. You will see this choice when you start to set up your page. In order to use this option, you must already have a live Amazon page, which must first be approved by Amazon. If you don't have one, don't let it stop you. I definitely prefer the list of products as a landing page, as it is the shortest path to the "Buy" button vs. a brand page. However, there are a few instances where the brand page might be worth testing to see how it performs. If you are trying to reach very broad keywords like "Camera Accessories" or "gifts for Dad," then it might help customers to go to your page and shop the categories on a brand page—provided you have done a good job of merchandising your Amazon page! However, the Amazon brand page does NOT look like the SERP page that customers expect to see, and it forces them to perhaps click or scroll more than the SERP page. But if you have a cool, visually interesting and engaging brand page and you think that showcasing your brand and catalog of products could work here, then try it out.

The third option you'll see for a place to send ad-clickers is a Custom URL. This is a custom SERP page within Amazon.com and essentially yields the same end result as adding your products (as outlined earlier in the "Create a Page" method); it's just a different way to get there. You can curate a page on your own by compiling the ASINs of the products you want to show. Although to pick your own products, it is easier to use the "Add" method discussed earlier. I have noticed one benefit of using the Custom URL method: you can pick *any* of your products. Amazon can designate some items ineligible and you cannot select them in the "Create a Page" method, but you can drop in the ASIN for a custom URL and that same item will appear! If you want to use this method, here's how to get the URL for a page:

Open another Amazon.com page, in addition to the AMS page you in which you are working. In the search bar on Amazon.com, first enter an ASIN of a product you want to display, then enter the "pipe" symbol, | Then enter the next ASIN, and a | and so on. After you have entered the ASINs of all the products you want to include, click the Search icon.

The page should show all the products of ASINs you entered. Copy the URL that was generated in your browser, and paste it in the spot for your Landing Page. Make sure to use the preview tool to make sure you copied and pasted correctly!

TIP: If you wanted to include products from a brand outside your own, you may be able to do so, but you might need approval from someone inside Amazon.

To sum up this section, here are the Pros and Cons of each Landing Page option:

Create a Page
Pro: Quick & easy. Can order products in the sequence you want.
Con: Some products might be ineligible. May accidently select other seller's products.

Amazon Brand Page
Pro: Could be an approach for some types of ads, can creatively and visually merchandise your products.

Con: Adds an extra step in the buying process. A brand page isn't what shoppers expect to see.

Custom URL

Pro: Can add products that are ineligible when adding from the tool.

Con: Can't set the order the products appear. Takes a little longer to set up.

FYI: If a shopper clicks on a product or ad and then clicks the back button, they may be served with another ad.

TYPES OF SEARCH CAMPAIGNS

I recommend separating your campaigns by the keywords you are using. I don't want to overcomplicate this, BUT it really is hard to pin down what element of a campaign is working when you lump all keywords into a single campaign. Branded terms usually convert the best, non-branded terms second-best, and competitive terms the worst. When you separate campaigns by keyword type, then you can better analyze them and see what is driving sales, what is driving clicks but not sales, etc. Within that framework, you will want to probably separate by product as well, especially if you have a lot of products on Amazon and they don't all have the same keywords associated with them. A consistent naming convention is key to keeping this all straight!

In the Yum Co cookie cutter example, a "cookie cutter" keyword (which is a non-brand keyword) may convert well (that is, get people to click the coveted "Buy" button), but the branded term "Yum Co Cookie cutter" would probably convert even better, thus having a higher conversion rate and higher Return on Ad Spend (ROAS). This is because the shopper who gets on Amazon and searches for a "Yum Co Cookie cutter" knows what she wants and just needs to find it. An ad that sends her right to a Yum Co Cookie Cutter item is not a stretch.

Conversely, if a shopper types in a term for a competitor, "CCC Cookie Cutter" (a competitor branded term Yum Co bid on) she is much less likely to change her mind and click on that "Yum Co Cookie cutter" ad. Keywords using competitive words typically would have a low conversion rate and low ROAS compared to branded keywords and non-branded keywords. That's ok, because they serve a different purpose—in some cases a shopper might type that "Acme cookie cutter" term Yum Co bid on, and the shopper is shown the amazing set of seashell cookie cutters! She likes them better than the Acme cookie cutter she had in mind and clicks the "Buy" button. This is the best-case scenario, and a good reason why you should employ competitive terms as part of your ad mix.

KEYWORDS

There are lots of ways to find keywords. This is very similar to other PPC Search Ads: if you have Google Ads, you'll definitely know the drill. Begin with the words that you already know are related to your product. That's pretty easy. Amazon will also suggest keywords related to your product as you build out your ad. You will want to think carefully about whether those keywords are right for that particular campaign, as they might be better suited to a different campaign (such as a non-branded campaign or a branded campaign). See Appendix A for a fun, easy exercise to use to develop keywords.

MATCH TYPE

Amazon allows you to choose "Exact" or "Phrase" match types when you add your keywords. Phrase match type matches what a shopper types in with your keyword plus other words before and after it. For example, if a shopper typed in "blue kids rainboots" and you bid on "rainboots" with a Phrase match type, then you could bid on that search. Conversely, if you do Exact match type and someone types in "blue kids rainboots" a keyword of only "rainboots" would not match.

Let's look at the Pros and Cons of each type:

Exact Match:
Pro: Super targeted, no clicks wasted on irrelevant searches, usually cheaper aCPC.
Con: Smaller audience, takes longer to develop list of keywords.

Phrase Match:
Pro: Reach a wider audience, quicker to compile list of keywords, scoops up shoppers who search with variations you haven't thought of.
Con: Could pay for irrelevant clicks, usually more expensive to bid on general keywords.

> **FYI: Both match types ignore the white space between search words.**

Misspellings are big. That, in my experience, has been a huge driver of sales, and usually at a lower aCPC since bidding on these words is less obvious. Just taking a letter out, slightly misspelling or thinking about how people would type if they were sounding it out phonetically can make all the difference. These misspellings can be really a gold mine because sometimes, they have less traffic as people aren't thinking to [bid 06:20] on that. Think really creatively. If you already know your business pretty well, you probably have a good keyword list. If you're just starting out, just start jotting keywords down and think about all the different ways your product is used in conversation. Talk about your product with others outside the business and listen to what they call your item. Also, think about regional differences. The people in the Northeast call something different than people out West. What's the slang for it? What are your competitors saying in their ad copy or descriptions? What if someone didn't know the name for your product—how would they describe it? Remember, many people use Amazon as starting point; as a search engine when they do not know what they are looking for exactly.

Back to campaign structure. You can set up your campaigns in a number of ways, but the most conventional way to do it is: Non-brand, Competitive and Brand. I think this stems from how a lot of people set up Google accounts. To name these, decide on a standard way to name across all campaign types. The name should include: 1) product or product category advertised, 2) the ad type, and 3) the ad sub-type. For example: Cookie Cutters_SEARCH_NON BRAND.

TIP: You can save your ad as draft at any time and come back to finish later. It will appear at the

> **top of the dashboard when you are ready to keep working.**

REAL WORLD EXAMPLE

Here's an example of the three categories of keywords for an existing product on Amazon. Let's look at the Fujifilm Instax Mini Instant camera (of which I have no affiliation nor have I ever worked with). If you were in charge of this product, here are some Non-brand words you could add to your campaign:

Camera

Instant camera

Instant print film camera

Print on demand camera

Print out pictures camera

> **Tip: You can use Spanish translations, French translations, any other translations for the most common non-brand terms.**

Non-brand campaigns are usually the most expensive, but you have the most search volume and thus, more sales opportunity. The targets for these should be different from your other campaigns, or at least they should be analyzed separately. These are the most basic, generic words to describe your product. In the Instax example, it would be "camera." As you can imagine, there are thousands of vendors on Amazon who sell camera and camera-related products, toy cameras, web cams, security cameras, etc. So, unless you are prepared to compete with those types of companies, you should get a little more specific to try to drive the bulk of your traffic. On a side note, I would personally still add "camera" to my campaign, but I would set it at a low max CPC that I could afford. You never know what other vendors are doing, so there could be an opportunity where you would get placement at that low CPC.

After all the learnings and exhaustive keyword exercises, thinking though slang, translations, etc., I will share a secret! In my experience, 99% of your traffic will come from the most basic words used to describe your item. In the Instax example, it would be likely "instant camera." So, why do this? If you plan to advertise on Google or Bing at some point, it's a worthy exercise to do because you will need the keywords then. It may also help you refine your product descriptions. After the Headline Search campaigns launch, you might notice some of the keywords getting more impressions than others (meaning people are using the terms to search), and you can use these to help with formulating your copy and SEO on your website.

Adding lots keywords does not hurt or cost anything to the campaign. If the keywords don't convert over time, Amazon may pause them, but that won't affect your campaign since those words weren't helping anyway. If that happens in your campaign, don't worry; look for other words that might convert better. The heart of this book, the key message, is that you don't know *until you test*. I added a silly misspelling that I felt was a stretch to one of my campaigns and it ended up being the 3rd best-performing keyword in the whole campaign. Let that lesson hold and you will find some great nuggets along the way! You never know until you test, and spending a little time to build out your keyword list will be worth the effort to get those learning about how people are searching for your products once your campaigns are up and running

If you do already have a comprehensive list of keywords from AdWords or other PPC, then just separate them by the campaign types you are using and then you can actually upload them right into Amazon (as long as it's in .xls, .csv, .tsv, or xlsx formats). You can also simply copy/paste a list straight into the tool.

TIP: **Amazon will actually tell you if a keyword is high, medium, or low traffic when you add it to your campaign.**

Ok, that whole section is one type of campaign in itself. Another type is a Competitive Terms campaign. This campaign's purpose is to try to woo shoppers who are looking for competitor models. To get started quickly, you just copy a Non-Branded Search campaign you've already created and change the keywords to Competitive Terms. Again, to avoid confusion, a consistent naming convention is critical. I would title it something to the effect of *YourProduct_SEARCH_Competitive* or *YourProduct_Comp_Search*. Remember, once you create a title, it is stuck, so double check that it correctly describes the campaign you are creating! I even do the type of campaign in all-caps, because it really does help you quickly see in the dashboard what type it is.

Here are some terms I would add if I were creating a competitive campaign for the Instax:
Polaroid
Polaroid Instant camera
Kodak Instant camera
Prynt

Impossible camera

Insignia camera

A competitive term can cost you a lot of money very quickly, and these convert the worst (in my experience I have only seen one campaign that actually does ok with competitive terms). So, why do competitive terms convert so poorly? The people who are searching for a specific item by brand already usually have a purchase in mind. For example, you have already read an article online about the Mini Instax and you want to check it out. When you search, you may see some other brands, but you came to Amazon to check out the Instax and that is what you are likely to do. Of course, there is *always* a chance that a shopper will see your ad and decide "forget the Instax, this Surerpints Camera looks amazing" and will click on your ad. That is why I keep competitive campaigns running at all times, however, I do it with very little budget and a low CPC bid. These ads generally do not perform well, but every now and then I will get a sale that will more than pay for the past few weeks of very low spend. The key is to keep the bids low enough that I am not running up a huge expense for those that do not convert. When I say low, I mean $5-$10 in spend a week. Yes, you can keep campaigns running that low and still get your brand out there when people search for your competitors. So, even if you are not always converting, this is very cheap advertising on the world's largest online store! Also, there is no ceiling on the amount of campaigns you can have, so you don't need to worry about using up any sort of quota!

> **Tip: Amazon does not allow the characters <>()#@^!* in keywords**.

Two down! Now, here's an option for a third. If you aren't in a very competitive category and your products already rank first when shoppers type in your brand, you may opt to skip this campaign type. Conversely, if you are in a highly competitive product category, you might already have competitors bidding on *your* brand name and product name. You can stop this by jumping in yourself with a Branded Search campaign. The good news is that you should have strong conversion on these ads, as shoppers who are typing in your brand probably already have a strong interest in your product. The bad news is that you will be paying shoppers that you previously got for free. However, the even worse news is that your competitors get the sale instead of you.

If you decide to launch a Brand campaign, then you can copy the Non-Brand campaign you already did, adjust the creative if desired and then remove all the non-brand keywords that are in there and replace them with branded terms. Following the Instax example, here are sample Brand campaigns:

Fujifilm
Instax
Instax mini
Mini 800
Fuji
Fuji instax
Fugee Instax (misspelling)
Instax camera
Fuji camera
Instanx fuji (misspelling)

These terms are all associated with their specific brand and product, even if they are not spelled right. These are words someone would use when he/she has your product in mind and is describing it in the Amazon search engine. Remember to add misspellings and variations at this point as well. You may wonder why you should even do a brand campaign—you may be thinking, "When you type in my brand, we are already the #1 result." This is great, and you want to keep it that way! Imagine how you would feel if your #1 competitor (or a new competitor you didn't even know about yet) bought YOUR brand name as a keyword and appeared on top of your search results. THAT alone is a great reason to run a Brand campaign.

WHY SO MANY CAMPAIGNS?

Why can't you just put all these words into one campaign? Well, you can. There is nothing stopping you for dumping all the keywords in one campaign, BUT it is really difficult to analyze the campaigns with a mix of keywords in the same place. Why? Because each type of word represents a different type of buyer and should have different KPIs. Even if you don't necessarily have different KPIs for each campaign, at least you will know what is driving sales and what terms are costing you the most money.

FYI: You can add up to 1,000 keywords per campaign!

SETTING YOUR BUDGET & BIDS

You have a couple of choices for budget. Unlike the Sponsored Products campaigns, you can choose the budget for the entire campaign *or* the daily budget. Either can work, so don't overthink it because you can *always* add budget later, although you can't take it away (you could pause or terminate the campaign instead). Your strategy should be to get the ads up and keep them going as long as you are meeting your ROAS goals. Having a daily budget may require a little more oversight, making sure you are not maxing out your budget too early and missing out on bidding on keywords at the end of the day (especially for shoppers on the West Coast). But if you are just testing the waters and want to start small, you can definitely ease into AMS Search Ads with the daily budget choice. This is also helpful if you know you only have a certain amount to spend in the 4th quarter for ads, no matter what happens with the ROAS. If that's the case, then click the dropdown to choose the budget "for entire campaign" and select your dates. Keep in mind the budget and spending for each campaign you create is completely separate. If you have a $100-spend-per-day cap on one Non-brand campaign, it does *not* include any spending on other Search campaigns or Sponsored Product/Product Display campaigns—those campaigns would operate under their own the per-day or per-campaign cap. Seeing aggregate data on actual daily or weekly spending is pretty tough through the dashboard alone. Each campaign is shown from its inception, not a standard date. So, you aren't comparing apples to apples when you look at spending on the Amazon dashboard of a campaign you set up in May and a campaign you set up in July. That's why I recommend setting up some Excel sheets and use something like my Snapshots method to better analyze the campaigns and see how much you are actually spending overall.

For Daily Budget, again, go easy on your first campaign's daily bid until you test the waters. Since you are likely bidding on non-brand terms as part of these ads, there can be significant search volume (Amazon.com is the fourth most-visited site on the internet), so a very generic term could 1) be expensive to win, and 2) have a ton of search volume (and in turn, get lots of clicks). Clicks are great as long as you are also getting some sales, so monitor closely after a few days and see what you are getting for the spend (if you are spending way more than anticipated and getting few sales, don't wait the full 14 days to pass before you lower the bids).

If you don't have a large budget to spend, don't worry! You can still participate in AMS, since many keyword average CPCs are below $0.50 (the absolute minimum is $0.10). You could have a two-week test (the minimum I would recommend, since the attribution window is 14 days) and spend only $20 a day ($280 budget total) and potentially get 40 clicks a day (if the average CPC is $0.50). Don't think you have to start with a six-figure (or even five-

or four-figure) budget to get a campaign up, running and bringing in sales!

You will ultimately set a bid for each keyword, and the more ubiquitous it is, the higher the bid should likely be. Not all keywords need to have the same bid. You might be really focused on winning the term "cookie cutter," but you don't care so much about "baking tools," so you would want to bid accordingly. Remember, you will only be charged one cent more than the next highest bid. Amazon will tell you the suggested bid, but you won't know until you really get into the campaign. Start a little lower than Amazon suggests and see how it does. If you are getting zero to few impressions then your bid is too low. Raise it a few cents and then monitor. If after raising the bid several times and not getting significantly more impressions and you know you aren't in a super-competitive category, then you likely have low search volume for those keywords. Find some new keywords or just make sure your campaigns are ready to go for when shoppers *do* use your terms. Then, just move on and try out other types of Amazon campaigns that might be better suited to generating demand in your product category.

Amazon recently launched a feature called "Estimated Win Rate" on some keywords that allows you to see how likely your bid is to win, even showing a 30-day median bid. This metric is refreshed every day and is not (at this time) available for every keyword. I have only seen it on the most popular search terms. You can adjust your bid up and down to change the likelihood of winning. This will take the guesswork out, and is very helpful when you are managing dozens of campaigns.

DATE RANGE

You also have to decide whether to set a date range or to just run the ad continuously at this point. Don't overthink this choice either, as you can always extend an ad or pause/terminate early if you like. You can even schedule ads to start at a later date. I think it's best just to leave them running, as long as you are checking in on the data every week and making sure spending is under control and ROAS targets are being met. Even if you might think you just want to run it through your season (if you have a seasonal product), don't! Keep those ads going in case people are searching off-season, and be ready to scoop up those sales. This isn't like running a TV commercial or print ad where you pay regardless of who is watching, you only pay when someone clicks. If you think you might need a campaign end date to perhaps prompt you to refresh your ads and take a deep dive into the analysis, then that is probably a good reason to select a campaign end date. However, I wouldn't go shorter than a quarter. You want to look at the campaign over team to glean as much as possible about how shoppers respond to your ads—IF they are responding. Don't let an underperforming ad run for a quarter! You can pause or terminate an ad at any time, whether it's a continuously run ad or one with a definite end date.

CREATIVE

Although the Creative section closes out this chapter, it is certainly not the least important by any means! It can get overlooked with so many other campaign elements to think about on your way down the page in creating the ad. Let it not be an afterthought, but use it as a tool to bring in the shoppers to your landing page to see your products. When I say "creative," there actually isn't too much room for creative liberties, but here's what you *can* do:

Brand Name: You can edit this slightly, if you want your brand to appear differently to shoppers from how it's pre-populated from your Amazon account. You have 30 characters.

Headline: Only 50 characters are allowed here! Not much space. If you have done Google AdWords before, you are probably a pro and can re-use some of your best-converting Headlines here. You have more characters for a full Google Ad, but you can apply the same principles with Amazon. If you are having writer's block, start with "Shop" and finish with what you are selling. (See Appendix C of this book for more writer's-block-busting Headline creation ideas.) I have seen major brands just use their brand name for their Headline! Yes, they repeated what is already shown. Remember, a "Sponsored by: Your Brand" is seen before the Headline. Please don't make this mistake!

"Shop our new Copper Cookie Cutters for easier baking." Just think about your product. Do not make unsupported claims or use all-caps. Amazon will reject those ads.

Next, you will select an image that will be the Featured image. According to Amazon, a product photo will outperform a brand logo here (which is what will probably be pre-populated). However, if your logo is recognizable to shoppers or you want to show it, I think you should test it. If not, let your product do the talking and upload a square .png file. Yes—you can upload an outside image here. You *cannot* do so in the next step for the product images.

Lastly, you will insert three product images. Pick your three best-sellers for widest in the category or product line you are advertising. These images are pre-populated by your image from the Amazon listing.

You can now preview your ad before you launch it. Amazon will auto-generate what the ad will look like and you can check it out. If you need a second opinion, use your snipping tool to snag that image and send it around to see what others think. You can click "edit" here to resize and move images around.

TESTING CREATIVE

To test a headline or image, create an ad with the first Headline and make sure your naming convention lets you know *which* creative it is, like *CookieCutters_Search_NonBrand_Option1*. Then launch the ad, then select "Copy." When setting up the copied ad, change the headline or image. Make sure you name it using the same naming convention, like *CookieCutters_Search_NonBrand _Option2* Then launch that one and see which one wins! Pause the losing ad and then try another ad and try to beat the results of the first. This is another reason to use Snapshots. It will allow you to easily compare ads that were created months apart.

You are now ready to hit "Submit ad for review."

AFTER THE CAMPAIGNS ARE RUNNING

After you start running your campaign, Amazon may pause certain keywords for various reasons. One reason is low click-through-rate. Remember, you can add as many keywords as you want. However, it is in Amazon's best interest to have shoppers click on ads, so they won't keep displaying your ad when shoppers clearly aren't clicking on it. If Amazon pauses a search term that you really want, then it's up to you to go back and change up the creative (Headline and image), which is the only lever you have to pull at this point. Amazon will not typically pause keywords that don't have impression, so your best bet is to try the keyword and see if it works.

REPORTING

It is difficult to get reporting info from the dashboard. The view is from the beginning of the campaign, not for a period of time that you select. So, to get the information you need to truly see how your campaigns are doing, you can either A) pull reports daily or weekly, B) create your own dashboard that you update weekly (I call this my Snapshots method), or C) pull the reports through a business intelligence. Option C would be ideal, but if you don't have access to that, then B is easy.

You can get keyword-level reporting by clicking into each individual campaign. You can even download these reports. However, the information accumulates from the beginning of the campaign, so you can't compare week to week or month over month. Skip to Chapter 6 to see how to easily fix this. These reports are good to see what is converting, and you should look regularly to adjust bids as needed.

In addition to keyword-level reporting, you can select a date range to download reports. These reports differ from the reports you can download in Headline Search Campaigns and Product Display campaigns…so you can't really use them to compare across campaigns—but if you want to see what info you can get from the reports, here's the scoop!

For these ads, you can choose the duration of the report. There is not a two-month limit like you see in Sponsored Products reports. This is just a daily report on what happened with the campaign on an overall level, not by keyword.

When you download the report, this is what you will see:

Date: These reports are by day, so you can see how this campaign performed on each specific day. All the following columns are metrics for that specific day.

Impressions: This is the number of people who were served your ad that day.

Total Clicks: Number of people who clicked on your product that day.

Click Through Rate: This is the click through rate, the impressions/clicks for that day.

Detail Page View: How many times a shopper viewed the product detail page for one of your products from the ad.

Total Spend: This is the amount you have spent on clicks for that day.

ACPC: Average cost per click. This is the average cost of all clicks that day.

Units Sold: Number of your products sold from that ad that day.

Total Sales: Sales in dollars of your products from that day from the ad.

ACoS: Advertising Cost of Sales. This number is calculated by dividing spend by sales. This is not the true cost, you must account for the price you sold your item to Amazon. I recommend taking the calculation a step further. Here's an example:

You make a product that retails on Amazon for $100. You sell it to Amazon for $80. When you see sales come through the dashboard or reports, you will see sales based on the $100 retail of $13,000. You spend $675 on ads. To truly see how the campaign is affecting your business, you should discount the sales by 20% and calculate your own Advertising Cost of Sales or ROAS calculation.

Net Sales Price $80/Retail price $100
= 0.80 or 80% of retail sales

($13,000 sales *.80 discount)/$675 ad spend
= $15.40 ROAS

You can slice and dice the report data any way you want but of course, its all about ROAS at the end of the day.

The deep-dive on Headline Search Ads is now complete. Now we can move to Sponsored Products.

Chapter 4 – Sponsored Magic

Sponsored Product ads are my favorite! They are pure magic—easy to run, quick as a wink to set up, and have the best ROAS compared to the other two ad types (in my experience). You don't need to worry about keywords at first (if you use the Auto Target option—more on that in a bit), and not of drop of copy or images are needed, nor a landing page to send customers. You just select the products you want to include in the campaign in a few clicks, title it and Amazon does the rest! Best of all, the minimum spend is $1. For a day! You can dip your toe in the Amazon ads waters for a very small price and a potentially big reward.

Similar to the Search Ads, the Sponsored Product Ads are also only pay-per-click. These ads are also keyword targeted. The beauty of these ads, in my opinion, is the sneakiness of them...many of them don't look like ads. These ads appear below the search results (not the top of the page like Search Ads) on desktop and mobile abased are looking for on Amazon. In addition, on the product detail page, a band of Sponsored Products appears below "Customers who bought this item also bought" so, it actually kind of looks like pictures of products other people bought—I myself have seen Sponsored Product Ads and took a few seconds for me to realize they weren't the "Bought this..." products even though all Sponsored Products Ads are designated "Sponsored." The ads served are based on customer search terms and relevance.

I have also seen another band of these ads at the bottom of the page (several pages of them)—in a recent look, I counted 14 products visible without any scrolling. This means there is lots and lots of inventory for these ads, and thus better ACPCs. With Headline Search Ads, there is only one opportunity per search result, but for Sponsored Products, there are around 14 spots visible and perhaps another few dozen if you click the arrows to scroll to the left!

GETTING STARTED

Because there are absolutely zero creative elements, Sponsored Product Ads are the quickest to set up and have best returns (that I have seen), so start with those.

Login with your AMS Vendor ID and select your brand from the top dropdown box (only applicable if you have more than one brand associated with your account). Then click on the "New Campaign" box in the upper left corner.

Choose the "Sponsored Products" selection. Move down to the "Choose Your Products to Advertise" section. Your brand should be showing and your items in the Amazon catalog. If you have multiple brands, all your items might show up here, giving you quite a few to sort through. Here's where you need a plan. I recommend very first starting a "Catalog" Search Campaign or some might call it an "ASIN Dump." Then you can just select all of your brand's products. Ineligible products will not have a clickable "Add" button. Select all the products you want to put in the campaign by clicking "Add." You also have the option to "Add all on this Page." The campaign summary on the right will show you what has been selected. For a catalog campaign, you would want to just select them all, but if you are in doubt about adding one—go ahead and add it, you can pause it later. If you know that sometimes you do

69

not have the "Buy" box when you go out of stock and a reseller might have it, check the product to be sure. You may not want to fund a reseller's ad campaign!

I recommend adding all your products, because before the campaigns start, you don't know exactly which ones will do well. Let the campaigns run awhile and see which items generated the most sales—the outcome may surprise you (if you have a catalog with several items). *That* is when you split them out and grow your campaigns.

Scroll down to the "Choose Your Campaign" settings. Here is the all-important name! Remember, you can *never change this name*, so choose wisely.

Naming

You could name it *FullCatalog_Sponsored Products_AutoTarget* or *CatalogSponAuto*. Here's my reasoning:

Full Catalog: You are advertising your full list of products. You could do *AllProducts*, *ALL_ASINS* etc. and later use this naming convention and narrow it down accordingly for assortments or categories when you break out campaigns (for example, Lenses)

Sponsored Products: The type of campaign it is. The three campaigns are NOT the same and need to be evaluated differently, so make sure you include what campaign *type* it is in the title. Remember: The campaigns you are creating now will be in the same dashboard as the other ad types.

AutoTarget: This means you are letting Amazon target people based on keywords. If you plan to use your own keywords, you need to note it: ManualTarget.

TARGETING

Then you actually choose if you want to do Manual or Auto Targeting. When you choose Auto, Amazon does the work for you and targets shoppers based on their search terms and matches up your product based on its description. Keep in mind, Amazon will probably be better at this than you, so let them do it at first. After all, it is in their best interest for a customer to click on your ad, so they are going to be good at targeting! This is where hidden keywords can come into play; you can use this feature to add words that might match to your products (like competitors' brands) that you don't want your customers to see. Once you have chosen Manual or Auto Target, you cannot change this. If you do want to change your mind here, you will have to terminate the campaign and start again (although the campaign will still show in your dashboard).

Auto Target Keywords:
Pro: Easy, quick, Amazon does the work for you. Allows your campaigns to target words you may not have thought of, helps you figure out which keywords convert.
Con: Can't pause keywords that aren't converting, can't increase bids on keywords that are converting, can't add any additional keywords, loss of control after campaign starts.

Manual Keywords:
Pro: Can focus on keywords that convert, can pause keywords that don't convert, can add keywords to the campaign at any time, can set keyword bids individually.
Con: Takes longer to set up (adding the keywords, setting individual bids).

My recommendation:
As I will dig into later on in the chapter, the best method is to start with Auto Targeting, so you can see what keywords are converting and then put those into *another* campaign. Then go back and adjust your bids as needed. This is because once a Sponsored Products Auto Target Ad has started, there aren't any levers to pull to improve performance: you can't

change creative/copy (because there isn't any) and you can't add to or pause the keywords. You can pull reports and look at what keywords drove sales, but there is nothing you can do with that information to alter your campaign. You can adjust the bid, but it adjusts it for *all* the campaigns, not just the ones that are working or not working. In contrast, in a Manual Targeted Sponsored Product campaign, you can go in and adjust bids based on a keyword's individual performance. You can also add new keywords or pause the ones that don't convert. You can also go in and add seasonally appropriate keywords when needed. I don't want to put down Auto Target campaigns too much, as those do a phenomenal job in getting you started quickly and figuring out what keywords *do* convert. So, start with Auto Target, then use the learnings and move to Manual.

BUDGET

After you have established your target method, next you set your average daily budget. The budget on Sponsored Products works differently from Search Ads. Here, you are only looking at a day at a time vs. a set overall campaign budget. You can select a budget as small as $1 a day. If the budget runs out during the day, your ads will no longer show. You can change your budget at any time, but I recommend you start small any time you are trying a new ad platform. Because of the volume on Amazon, you can see very quickly the pace your campaigns will take. Sales do take up to three days to show, so whatever budget you start with, commit to it for at least five days to really get a picture of how it's going. The spend numbers post faster than the sales numbers, so try not to get too anxious in the first couple days if you see zero sales. You can start with a very small budget. If you only have $50 to test, start with $10 a day. As tempting as it may be to pull the plug after two days with no sales, wait at least until that 72-hour mark and evaluate then.

Next, you set your duration. You have two options: choose a date range or run continuously. I'll confess...I have only selected "run continuously!" Since you can pause or terminate the campaigns at any time, my thinking was—why not? On all my campaigns, I am trying to hit a particular ROAS target based on the brand or product/product group. So, I like to just keep them running continuously. If an ad is not performing, I will take it down regardless of the time of an arbitrary campaign length (after I gave it a few weeks, at least). The reason I could see someone using the campaign start and end date is to tightly control the budget. If you are not working on a ROAS target model and you know you only have a finite amount to spend, then choose this option.

For example, you sell pencils online and have been given an ad budget of $500 for a campaign. Your product, not surprisingly, has a sales spike in August/September, so you decide to run your campaign from August 1 to October 1. Since this is 62 days, you could budget about $8 a day and then never go over your campaign budget….You *could* do this, but I disagree with this methodology for a few reasons. First, you don't 100% know when the sales volume is at its peak (although you may know generally), and arbitrarily spreading out the budget evenly might cause you to run out of budget on days that you have a high search volume. I have heard of situations where you might have daily budget for the East Coast shoppers, but then when the West Coast gets home and is shopping while watching Netflix at night, the budget could be gone and no one will be seeing your ads. I have not seen a great system for alerting low budget throughout the day, so if you are spending your max budget every day, you should increase it. That being said, only increase your budget if it is profitable for you. As I have said before, there is so much search volume on Amazon, it doesn't take long to see if a campaign is working— meaning if people click on your ads and then buy your product. If your ads aren't being clicked on— you aren't paying, so you can just hold tight. If you are getting quite a few clicks, but no sales, then the problem is your product page. It's not necessarily the price, as shoppers know this before they click. But you might want to audit your PDP for how you present your product details, images, etc.

Back to the pencils example. If you set up your Sponsored Product Ad and you are making $750 a week for about $64 spent, then your ROAS is 1171.88%! All signs point to get more budget! Keep spending! Whatever you do, DON'T SHUT IT OFF! Don't just keep that same $436 you have left, bump up your daily budget and monitor the weekly progress. As long as you have inventory to sell through Amazon and you are hitting ROAS target (1171.88% is above any target a Finance department could set), don't stop! This is where it is so important to have that net sales price so you can calculate an accurate ROAS, and you truly know how much you can spend while maintaining profitability.

Next, you need to set your CPC. Amazon uses an action-based pricing model, so that means you will pay $0.01 above the next highest bidder. The minimum you can bid for these ad types is $0.02. If you decide you want your CPC to be $0.60 and the other person bidding for that keyword has a max CPC at $0.30, then you will only pay $0.31. Yay! Conversely, if your max CPC is $0.60 and another competitor bid $0.75, his product will be shown (paying $0.61) and yours will not. We will talk more in-depth about this in Chapter 6, but a weekly analysis is the best way to see movement on your campaigns from week to week. If a week goes by and you haven't spent any money, then you are being outbid. In some weeks, you might still get sales because of the 14-day attribution window, but it was because your product ads showed *last* week, not *this* week. It's hard to glean that type of information from the current AMS dashboard.

Now, grab a cup of coffee because your ad will be live in about an hour!

After the catalog campaign is up and running, you should give it a couple of weeks and just analyze it before you jump into others. Once you start to see which products are selling, then you can split out by item categories and/or start some Manual Target campaigns. Yes, you can have numerous Sponsored Products campaigns (remember how much inventory there is for ads!).

SPONSORED PRODUCT CAMPAIGN STRUCTURE EXAMPLE

Here's a way you could structure your Sponsored Products campaigns. Let's say you sell gourmet specialty foods, and you have about 75 products listed on Amazon. For your first campaign (titled like

"Catalog_SponsoredProd_Auto"), you added your whole catalog of food items: jelly, candy, cheese, baking mixes. You noticed a jelly ASIN and a candy box are selling the best, making up 40% of all campaign sales. You decided to break-out a campaign of jellies to increase the performance even further. You repeat the same step as you did for the Catalog Campaign, but only add your 10 jelly SKUs (naming it "Jellies_SponProd_Auto"). You can always add a product later if you have a new launch, or delete one if you make a mistake. This campaign does wonderful, and you are selling a ton of your top jelly products. After you see how that campaign does, you could divide even further and have a campaign of large jars ("18ozJellies_SponProd_Auto") and sampler packs ("SamplerJellies_SpronProd_Auto"), etc. There will be a bit of trial and error based on your business and the market. You never really know what will bubble up, so here are some ways to separate campaigns:

By size (6 oz. jars of jelly)

By sets (various gift sets)

By category (jellies)

By accessories (e.g., camera accessories)

You realize after creating a few more campaigns that your chocolate-dipped pretzels aren't selling at all from the ads. You could then isolate them in a new campaign and see how they do with increased opportunity to get exposure. Each campaign is an opportunity for more exposure, and remember that there is plenty of inventory for ads. As long as you can keep track (you'll need to implement something like the Snapshots method or similar), you should definitely create more Sponsored Products Ads. You could have 3 or 30 depending on the size of your catalog and how the ads perform. 30 ads will take some work to set up, but it will be worth the effort!

As you have seen on the dashboard, there is a "Copy" option under the far right column (labeled "Actions"). We discussed in Chapter 2 how you can quickly start a new campaign this way. For Sponsored Products campaigns, you can do this as well. If you decide to Copy, you'll need to change the items in the campaign, CHANGE the name (the default will be the campaign name that you copied plus the numeral "1"), and check any other settings. Then, you can just save and you are good to go! Again, not a huge time saver, but if you know you are not going to change most of the settings, it may help a little.

You can stop reading this chapter here and it is very possible to have incredible success on AMS! Sponsored Product Ads really are that simple. When I first started working with the Amazon Marketing Services platform, a Marketing Agency was charging a 6% commission to run these Sponsored Auto-Target campaigns....no way! These campaigns are really too easy to justify a commission. For Headline Search Ads where you have some creative to take care of, and where you're curating landing pages and selecting keywords, then an expert can bring some value (although you can easily do this yourself, too), but under no circumstances should you pay a commission on an ad campaign THIS easy to run!

So, as I said, you can stop here.... However, if you have the time or want to see if your results can get even better, stay with me! You can run campaigns all day long and just use Amazon's Auto Target and will still have the opportunity to be plenty successful—but if you *do* want to try to take the campaigns a bit deeper and set yourself up for better success in the long run, then definitely move on to Manual Targeting.

If you have been running some Sponsored Products Auto Target Ads for a couple of weeks, a good practice here is to pull a report and look at the keywords that are driving your Sponsored Product sales already. To pull these reports, click into an individual campaign and select the "Reports" tab. Then you can select the date range of the report you want. I recommend the widest date range possible—the more data, the better. However, Amazon will only allow you to select within the previous 60 days. This is another reason to get your Snapshots done each week/biweekly. You cannot look back and get this data later (over 60 days), so get in the habit of grabbing it, and consider maybe even setting a reminder to yourself to pull a report regularly.

The reports may take a few minutes to generate and when they are ready, click "download" and you can open it in a .csv file. These reports can easily be several thousands of lines long—each click is a line on this report. I do not pull these weekly….this could definitely be an option for your reporting, but I have found my Snapshots method easier—especially since I need to analyze several dozen campaigns. If you do want to use these reports instead of Snapshots, you'll still have to tinker with the spreadsheet a little after you have downloaded them. Going in to each campaign and downloading individual reports, sorting, formatting, etc.? No way! However, periodically pulling the reports is still valuable for getting keywords. Let's look at what data you get when you download a report.

Here are the columns you will see, from left to right (all the numbers are related to the time period of that report):

Campaign: This is the name of your campaign that you chose.

81

Keyword: This will have an * in the cell if it is an Auto Target report, and a keyword you added to the campaign if it is a Manual Target report.

Customer Search Term: This is what you are looking for! What the shopper typed in the search box that matched up with your keyword (Manual Target) or Amazon chose for you (Auto Target)

First Day of Impression: The date of the first time a shopper is shown the ad from a particular keyword as it relates to the time period of this report.

Last Day of impression: The date of the last time a shopper is shown the ad from particular keyword as it relates to the time period of this report.

Impressions: This is the number of people who were served your ad for that search term.

Clicks: Number of people who clicked on your product from that search term.

CTR: This is the click through rate, the impressions/clicks. Not a really significant metric on this report. This might not mean a lot here, as some search terms have so few impressions, a high click through rate may not mean that much.

Total Spend: This is the amount you have spent on clicks for that particular search term in that campaign.

ACPC: Average cost per click. This is the average cost of all clicks for that keyword

Orders placed within 14 days of a click: This number refers to units, and it counts all product sales of the product shown in the ad that were bought by a shopper and anything else within your brand who saw an ad no more than 14 days ago. Here's an example:

If you searched "food gifts" and saw a yummy jar of jelly which happened to be a Sponsored Product Ad that you clicked on, checked out but didn't buy it—but then you came back 10 days later and decided to buy it, that original "food gifts" line would get the credit.

These orders ALSO include other items in your brand. So, in the gourmet food example, the search term was "food gifts" and you clicked on the 14 oz. jar of pepper jelly. However, the reviews said it was too spicy, so you decided to buy a jar of the raspberry jam instead. Or you bought the pepper jelly and then decided to buy raspberry jam, too. In both scenarios, the sales of the raspberry jam would be included here.

Product Sales within 14 days of a click: This is the same line as the previous, but in dollars instead of units. Is the sum of all brand products that were sold from clicking on that product ad.

Conversion Rate within 14 days of a click: This is calculated from orders/clicks. Like the CTR, there may not be a lot of data in some of these lines and the results look a bit skewed.

Advertised SKU units ordered within 14 days of click: Now we're looking at just the actual SKU that the customer clicked on and how many jar of Pepper Jelly specifically where sold from the each specific term

Same Brand SKU units ordered within 14 days of click: These are the number of units sold (dipped pretzels, popcorn tins, etc.) that were bought instead of OR in addition to the Pepper Jelly.

Advertised SKU Product Sales within 14 days of click: These are the sales dollars from the *units* sold.

Same Brand SKU Product Sales within 14 days of click: These are sales dollars of all the *brand* sales from that search term.

Looking at data in a spreadsheet the way it looks when you first download it quickly gives me a headache, so I immediately do a few things to make it useful. First, I sort it by sales in descending order. Now you can quickly look at the biggest elements of the camping and find out what is moving the needle. There could be tens of thousands of lines in this report and the majority are irrelevant! You can analyze yourself to an early grave, if you look at every line, so please keep in mind quantity on some of these impressions. Don't spend time analyzing the bottom of the list where the volume is so little. Focus on the top (and in my opinion, don't really focus on this spreadsheet at all).

Now, if you have the time, you could forget the Snapshots method and just analyze from there. You could pull the report from the previous week, or however you want to look at it, then quickly see your sales and what you spent. There are two main problems with this method: First, you are still going to have to get in to another spreadsheet (unless of course, you have a business intelligence system that can pull these numbers). Say you pull Week 1 and analyze your data from that campaign. Now, next week you will have to pull the same report and then build another table to compare the two from the previous time period and to see trending over time. Then you would still have to add a column to calculate your true ROAS based on the cost you sold to Amazon. These downloadable reports are great, but they still don't tackle what is missing that you as a vendor need: time-based comparisons and a *true* ROAS. Also, requesting and downloading reports, then formatting them each week can take a really long time if you have manual reports. Since I typically have several dozen campaigns running simultaneously, it is much quicker to just get the snapshots and quickly copy that data into the tables I have already created. I'm sure there are other workarounds that you could come up with, too!

I typically pull these reports every few weeks to look at the keywords that are converting. If it was my full-time job to run AMS, I would probably dig a little deeper, but AMS is just a fraction of what I do, so I don't have the time to dig in too deeply each week. I usually keep it high-level and focus on what matters most: the money-makers!

Manual Targeting

Manual Targeting Sponsored Product campaigns work the same as their Auto Target counterparts, except that they require a bit more work from you. Using those reports you pulled, here is a good place to see which keywords are converting into sales. You can do a few things with this info—first, if it's a word you didn't think about, then definitely add that word over in the appropriate AMS Search campaign (Brand, Non-brand, or Competitors) and also add it to any other PPC search you might be doing. Then you can create even more Sponsored Product Ads with these keywords. Just like with Search campaigns, you will need to separate the keywords by type. Here's an example of a name:

"Jellies_SponProducts_ManualTarg_NonBrand."
Long? Yes! But will it save confusion and headache later? I hope so! As with Headline Search Ads, it will be harder to analyze and compare the campaigns if all the keywords are in only one campaign. Breaking them out by type will be a little more work upfront, but makes things much easier later on. In short, the payoff is worth the initial effort!

To start a Manual campaign, perform the same actions as discussed above under the Auto Target section, but select "Manual Targeting" instead of "Auto." Move down to "Add keywords and bids." This is similar to the Search Ads in that you are selecting specific keywords and setting individual bids. This is different from Search Ads in that you are using these keywords to send shoppers to one specific product *page*, not a curated product *list*. You can check out Amazon's suggested keywords or add your own. The best list is where you add the words you have gotten from Amazon in previous Sponsored Products Auto Target campaigns that you already know convert well. Again, make sure you change the name to one that makes sense; the auto-generated name Amazon gives you will not tell you what the campaign is promoting.

Remember, non-branded keywords can get very expensive, very fast! If you sell sewing scissors and bid on a high-search volume word like "scissors," then expect to run up a big bill by the next morning. You risk wasting clicks on shoppers searching for kids' scissors and hair-cutting scissors, plus the CPC will be very high. Start with more specific keywords, and if you do use a broad keyword, rein in your CPC until you see how competitive the keyword is. In this type of Sponsored Product Ads, each keyword is bid on individually. You also have the same options for matching as with Headline Search ("Exact" or "Phrase"), plus another "Broad" match option. Phrase match type matches what a shopper types in with your keyword *plus* other words before and after it. Exact match matches on that exact keyword *only*, and is the most restrictive. Broad match is the least restrictive (meaning you will get the most traffic from these), as it matches the keyword with close variants, like the plural/singular form, acronyms or abbreviations.

Bid+ is another featured of Sponsored Products Manual Targeted Ads. Bid+ is a newer feature that increases the chance that your ad will appear at the top row of search result pages. To use this feature, click into the campaign and then on the Campaign Settings tab. You can select Bid+ to permit Amazon to increase your CPC bid by up to 50% for the ads that could appear in the high traffic placements, which are at the top of the search results page. Only test this feature on campaigns that have a healthy ROAS.

Congratulations, if you made it this far, you have pretty much exhausted the Sponsored Products Ads! You might want to stop here with these easy, high-ROAS ads, but if you want to go even further down the sales funnel on Amazon, let's jump to the most specific of the three: Product Display Ads!

Chapter 5 – Product Display Ads

I left Product Display Ads last for a reason. I classify these as Phase III ads. They can be the most complicated, and the two types of Display Ads are so dissimilar, it is curious to me why Amazon put them in the same Campaign Type. These ads are really two very different ad types. According to Amazon, Product Display Ads "target by product or interest." "Product" or "interest" are actually vastly different! So, let's discuss these ads in two separate sections: **Target by Interest** and **Target by Product**.

TARGET BY INTEREST

After the success and high ROAS I hope you are achieving with Sponsored Product and Search Ads, don't necessarily expect the same quick results with

Display Ads. This is particularly true of Product Display-Target by Interest campaign type, which I'll refer to as "Target by Interest" hereafter. Target by Interest ads are akin to prospecting—you are just looking for totally new customers, AND you are marketing to people who aren't even on Amazon! These ads appear in Amazon's Display Advertising Network. Stop and think about this for a second! This is a major distinction of these ads and it's a little hard to tell when you are setting up your ad. You may want to stop right here. If you are just getting started, and your goal is to sell more on Amazon, then it may make more sense to just keep your focus and dollars on customers who are at least already on the site. I would classify this as a Phase III tactic, for when you are up running and seeing some measurable results with Sponsored Product Ads and Search Ads, and have already begun to test Target by Product Ads (which I'll cover next). However, if you want to at least explore the Target by Interest campaign type, let's dive in.

Prospecting Shoppers

In these Target by Interest campaigns, you are marketing to people who are much farther up in the sales funnel. This requires more strategy, more budget and more patience than the set-it-and-forget-it Sponsored Products campaigns. That means these ads hit can people who aren't shopping for your item, and they typically have a very low ROAS. Prospecting ads target people who may just be reading about something related to your product, are not actively in-market for a product (unlike the most of the shoppers who you target in Sponsored Products and Search Ads). Of course, when looking for new customers, you may think: "Great! Let's do this, show my product to everyone on the internet!" However, what *can* happen—especially if you have a cool-looking product—is that you get lots of clickers (costing you money), but very few sales. If this is your strategy and are just looking for awareness, then by all means, use these types of ads. If you are more closely focused on hitting that ROAS target, then you may want to test drive a couple of these campaigns with a small budget and see how they do. You can start daily budget as small as $1 a day, so there is very little risk to test it. Remember to keep the ads running for at least a week before deciding how to proceed.

For Amazon's Target by Interest ads, you select from a list of several very broad interests, such as Home & Garden, Health & Beauty, Baby & Kids. So, there are no keywords at all. From there, you can drill down into more specific categories and select the ones you want. Keep in mind if you select just one or two, the audience might be so small that very few people may see your ad. This kind of defeats the purpose of prospecting, because you are looking for new customers. However, if you go *too* broad, then you risk paying for lots of clicks from not-so-serious shoppers. Again, just test it! One thing that is important to note is that you cannot change the interests selected once you set up your campaign. You can always copy the campaign and then add/subtract interests if your audience is too small or too wide when you first set up the campaign.

Like other AMS ads, Product Display Ads are simple to create as well! To start, click on "create a Product Display Ad." Next, choose a Targeting Method. Here, you can select Target by Interest (what we just covered) or Target by Product. Next, you select a product to advertise (you can only choose one here). The detail page of the product selected will serve as the landing page when the ad is clicked. Type in your model, ASIN, etc. and select your product. Next, choose interests for your campaign. Once you click on a category, it automatically expands into smaller categories. To add categories you want to target, just click them. You can add as many as you want, but remember there is no report that will tell you which category is driving the sales, so I recommend choosing a narrow category for each ad and so you know what is moving the needle.

When someone types in "Swinging Clubs Golf Bag" they are very interested in finding out more about that specific brand of golf bag. However, when a shopper has identified themselves as looking for "sports equipment," they may be looking for hundreds of other things *aside* from golf bags. They could be looking for hundreds of other things within the golf category itself.

Again, I recommend using the Snapshots method or a similar analysis method for evaluating these campaigns by week as well. You can, of course, download reports on these campaigns, too. The Product Display reports do not reveal too much—there is no transparency on where the ads are shown (in case you were wondering—which I certainly was!). These reports are different from the others, and they list performance by day as a line for each day. Here, you can see impressions, clicks, click-through-rate, detail page views, total spend, average CPC, units sold and ACoS. This report does not show brand sales, just sales for that specific product only.

I do think there is a time and place for prospecting in every marketing plan. However, it's important to be smart about it, and to *not* blow your budget on the worst-converting portion of your plan. Take it slow, especially if you don't have any PPC experience with prospecting. You could take a seasonal approach. For example, Sponsored Products and Search Ads will always keep plugging away all year and advertise those pencils to the odd customer that wants them off season. However, you may consider using Target by Interest in August when you *know* that is when millions of shoppers are actually looking for pencils—the ROAS should be better when you know a large number of people are potentially in-market for an item. This situation provides a better opportunity for efficient campaigns and fewer wasted clicks from shoppers who aren't in market. In another scenario, if you just released a new product and you want to target your specific category, this could also be part of an awareness/launch strategy to get your product out there.

If you have a large catalog, managing the ads here can become unmanageable. You are only advertising one product at a time, unlike Headline Search and Sponsored Products Ads where you can promote several at once. If you have 50 products in your Amazon catalog, then it could potentially be 50 different ads. Not to mention, if you want to test a different creative message or test various audiences, that will be even *more* ads. Once you create your ads, you cannot change the creative, you must create a new ad and then test it against the existing (control) ad. This is where the Copy action is so helpful. You just copy the ad you are already running, and then change an element of the ad, like the wording in the Headline. However, since you cannot select (yes, I'm bring this up again!) a date range in the overall dashboard, you will not be able to compare the old and new version of the ad side-by-side until you set up the Snapshots or another type of reporting.

You also cannot change targeted interests once the campaign is running, so if the "Camera, Photo & Video" (a choice Amazon provides) audience is not clicking or converting and you want to see how people in the "All Digital Cameras" group does, you will have to copy the "Camera, Photo & Video" campaign and then change the audience. This is also how you would change creative if you wanted to. These ads are all seen together in the same dashboard, so again, I think pulling them into Excel via API, my less-technical Snapshots method, or another way that works for your business, is a must to keep track of data.

This is only one part of Display Ads. The other side of Display Ads is completely different!

TARGET BY PRODUCTS

Target by Product ads are ads are placed on specific products on Amazon.com. Again, there are no keywords here. These ads show up on the product pages (PDP). They are usually seen on the right hand side of the page, underneath the "Buy" button on the product of the page you are visiting. They are a single product ad that you will need to write a Headline to promote (just as you would do for Target by Interest, above) and shown on a specific product you designate by ASIN. This is a different type of placement than the Sponsored Products Ads that are in the band across the page. You could classify these types of ads as Phase 2, as they are appropriate for use after you have mastered Sponsored Products and Headline Search Ads.

When I first started running these ads, I had little initial success. The first three products I tried to make work ended up costing more than they earned. However, when I tested a fourth product—a complementary product—bingo! I suddenly had a ROAS comparable to some of my Search campaigns. Since then, I have found a few conquesting ads that have met my ROAS targets, but they are the toughest nuts to crack. It has taken a lot of testing to find what works. I still use complementary product ads as much as possible.

You can boil Target by Product ads down to two (major) things: 1) you can conquest, and 2) you can target items you *think* your potential customers are also buying or looking at. Let's look at some examples:

Conquesting

This tactic comes into play when you have a head-to-head competitor you'd like to take sales from. Here's what happens: a customer searches for a specific Nikon camera and then another camera company bids on that search term, resulting in an ad on Nikon's product page. This is risky, as a customer who types in a specific product usually is pretty far down the road to purchase that product. The result is usually low click-through rates and even lower sales and ROAS. If conquesting is what you are looking for, though, this tactic is for you! However, don't be surprised if the product you conquest turns around and bids to conquest on *your* product page!

> **TIP: To get the most conversions, your product should have a lower price and better reviews than the product you are conquesting.**

RELATED PRODUCTS ADS

The example for this type of Product Display campaign that I have seen Amazon use is an ad for a helmet on a bike page. So, if you make cameras, you could test buying ads on crib ASINs or other baby-related keywords if your experience has told you that many expecting parents buy new cameras. Or, in a more direct connection, if you sell cell phone accessories, you would want to test buying ads on various cell phone ASINs.

To start a Product Display-Target by Product Ad, first choose the targeting method. Select "Product" and then select YOUR product that you would like to advertise. You can enter your model number or ASIN and then click "add" when you see the product you want. Do the same thing for the product you'd like the ad to *target*. If you want to run a Related Products Ad and you sell helmets, choose a bike ASIN. You can select specific products by ASIN or model or type in a broader category and click on the ones you want—as many as you want. There is also a checkbox for if you want to expand to other related products in addition to the ones you selected. If your item is only related to a few very specific items, do *not* select this box. You don't want to waste clicks on products that won't fit, won't match, or aren't compatible with your product. Next is the VERY important campaign name. But if you want to widen the audience, expand by all means. You could use a naming convention such as: "Helmet RTY998 PRODUCT DISPLAY RELATED." You want to make sure you can easily know which one of *your* products is advertised when you look at the dashboard. Also, you don't want to confuse this campaign with another conquesting or prospecting ad you may do.

Another option is targeting by related categories. In this option, Amazon serves your ad under the Buy Boxes in categories related to the item you are advertising. Amazon pre-selects the category matching your product and allows you to drill down slightly. This option will depend on what are you advertising. Again, if its very specific, you may not want to target all shoppers in a category. On the flip side, it will open up the ad to more shoppers.

Set your CPC next. Amazon will give you a suggested bid. The minimum bid is $0.02. I usually start lower and see if I can get any placement. If not, then I'll move up the bid up. Next, you suggest the date range, which I recommend running continuously like the rest. Now, you create your ad! Unlike Sponsored Products, you actually have room to call out features, etc. Of course, that also makes it all the more complex because you can test your message!

You will write your headline message. While there are a lot of ways to think about this, one idea is to make sure the headline conveys additional info from your product title. For example:

Your title is: Acme Adult Bike Helmet Model RTY0045

A sample Headline could be: Top-level protection and comfort

No need to waste characters reiterating that it is a bike helmet; the customer can see that in the product title.

At this point, you have the ability tweak your product description a little. You may have it a certain way for your PDP, but you can shorten or tailor it a bit at this point. For instance, you probably don't need the model number in the ad. You can change the name of your brand at this point, as well.

Using the prior example, you could shorten your product description to: Adult Comfort Helmet

Your logo will populate below and you can edit if needed. Amazon recommends using a PNG image. The image should be 100 pixels by 100 pixels, and the file *must* be less than 1MB. Then you can review the headline, image and logo in the preview of your ad in various configurations. There are about ten sizes/types of ads that can be rendered for this ad type. Click through them, and if you aren't happy, go back up and adjust the headline and/or title. The image of the product will be pulled from the PDP.

If you want to test different headlines, just use the "Copy" feature to copy the ad and then change the headline only. You will need to title it Version B or something to denote it. Make sure you keep a log to know which version is which since there's not a lot of room in the name of the ad to tell.

Remember: You are buying an ad on another product, so when people see your ad, it's because they had something else in mind first. You may not get a lot of conversion advertising a big ticket purchase on another big ticket purchase. You may do better if your product is a smaller accessory to the main item they are looking for (again, that's what the shopper was originally interested in). Just test, test, test! Do some formal or even informal research to determine what else your shoppers are buying and when they are buying it. You may get a much larger list of products than initially thought.

After you get your Product Display Ads set up and running for a couple of weeks, you should evaluate them against the Sponsored Products and Search campaigns. If you use the Snapshots method, you can easily compare ROAS across campaigns. If not, you'll have to build out some other custom reports, as the reports that Amazon spits out for you are not the same across campaigns. You may see the lower ROAS and opt to go with Sponsored Products 100%, or you may see a couple of campaigns running in Display that are performing pretty well and choose to keep those running and terminate or pause the rest. Since there is no end date (if you follow how I set them up), then it's up to you to keep a close eye on the performance before a bad ad gets out of hand in spending. If you have realistic budget limits set, you know what you are getting into.

Chapter 6 – Evaluating Your Campaigns

Everything is running, now let's dig into how the campaigns are performing. As mentioned, I like using ROAS as the main metric instead of Amazon's ACoS. However, I do have to "discount" the sales to the net invoice price that is sold to Amazon. Now I can see if I am making money! The "Sales" Amazon reports are its sales to customers at the retail price. As mentioned earlier (in Chapter 3), you *true* ROAS is *not* Sales/Spend. It would be if you actually received the full amount for the product, but as you know, you received what Amazon paid. So, you need to think about this and view all the campaigns through that lens. This could be set up many different ways depending on what your accounting department thinks is best. If you only sell one or two products to Amazon, this is pretty easy. Here's an example:

> You sell one super cooler on Amazon at a retail price of $300. Amazon pays you $200 for each cooler. You set up an ad campaign and sell 150 of them through Search Ads. So, your attributed sales as seen in the AMS dashboard are $45,000 (yes!). You spent $3,200 on ads to get these sales. The ROAS may appear to be $14.06 but this isn't the case. *Your* sales are only $30,000, so the *true* ROAS is $9.38. For reporting on an ongoing basis, you'd just discount your sales by 33% when you calculate your ROAS.
>
> 150 * $300 = $45,000 Amazon Sales
> 150 * $200 = $30,000 Company Sales using Net Invoice Price
> $200 / $300 = 66.67% Adjustment for Net Invoice Price
> ($45,000 * .67) / $3,200 = $9.38 ROAS

SNAPSHOTS

As I have mentioned many times before, AMS dashboards *do not* display data in one period of time relative to another time period. This is problematic

106

for a few of reasons. First of all, AMS says it is beneficial to leave the ads on, especially for Sponsored Products, in order to let the "machine learning" take place. This means the algorithm gets better and serves better ads for better conversions. Well, you can't really test that yourself if you only look at the dashboard, because you can't make those comparisons.

Say your product is highly seasonal, and you expect a couple of big sales spikes throughout the year and a consistent smaller baseline rate of sales the rest of the year. If you just leave your Sponsored Products campaigns on, then you can't tell how the ads are doing off-season vs. during-season by just looking at the dashboard. Sure, you could stop them all and then start them again, but that is a lot of work and you would lose the benefit of machine learning.

My Snapshots method isn't perfect, but it is a good way to quickly get around the dashboard reporting problem. A better way is if you have a resource at your company that can do an API call into the AMS reporting and then build a business intelligence dashboard to show you what you need and allow you to pull time periods you want. Unfortunately, most of us don't have that resource, so this is a low-tech hack to get the weekly/daily/monthly numbers you need!

The products you sell to Amazon probably all have differing rates of margin, and thus should really be evaluated differently depending on profitability. If you have a very large catalog of products, you may use a weighted average based on the percentage of sales of each product.

My low-tech hack is this: Each week (or whenever you determine makes the most sense for your business), take a "snapshot" of the AMS campaign dashboard, meaning pull some information from that point in time. Yes...this is a manual process, but it does do the job—so stay with me! With this snapshot, you will then need to set up a simple MS Excel or Google Docs spreadsheet. I am not clicking into each campaign in this method, just taking information directly from the dashboard. Once you have built a Snapshots spreadsheet, you will be able to copy it again for each campaign. I use three Excel books: one for Sponsored Products, one for Headline Search, and one for Product Display Ads. I then create tabs for each campaign. The structure of each is identical, because at the end of the day I am looking for the same thing: What was my ROAS last week?

The spreadsheet that I settled on is the most simplistic version, so I can update it as quickly as possible every Monday morning. With so many campaigns to evaluate, I just edited it down to the bare minimum columns and that gives me the essentials to analyze the campaigns' ROAS. For further analysis, I will download reports periodically and review keywords, etc., but for basic "what did we spend/what did we sell last week" purposes, I use Snapshots.

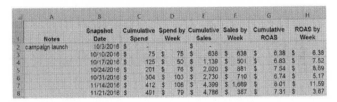

	A	B	C	D	E	F	G	H
	Notes	Snapshot Date	Cumulative Spend	Spend by Week	Cumulative Sales	Sales by Week	Cumulative ROAS	ROAS by Week
2	campaign launch	10/3/2016	$ -		$ -			
3		10/10/2016	$ 75	$ 75	$ 638	$ 638	$ 6.38	$ 6.38
4		10/17/2016	$ 125	$ 50	$ 1,139	$ 501	$ 6.83	$ 7.52
5		10/24/2016	$ 201	$ 76	$ 2,020	$ 881	$ 7.54	$ 8.69
6		10/31/2016	$ 304	$ 103	$ 2,730	$ 710	$ 6.74	$ 5.17
7		11/14/2016	$ 412	$ 108	$ 4,399	$ 1,669	$ 8.01	$ 11.59
8		11/21/2016	$ 491	$ 79	$ 4,786	$ 387	$ 7.31	$ 3.87

Sample Snapshots Sheet

The spreadsheet I use has eight columns:

- **Notes:** Where I notate any changes, events, things to remember about the campaign like: raised CPC bids, added keywords, etc.
- **Snapshot Date**: The date I copied the data from the AMS Dashboard. I do this on a weekly basis.
- **Cumulative Spend**: The spend number in the AMS dashboard for a particular campaign at the point of recording the data
- **Spend by Week**: Calculation of current week's cumulative spend minus last week's

cumulative spend. (In above screenshot, the calculation is: cell D5 = C5 – C4)

- **Cumulative Sales**: The sales number in the AMS dashboard for a particular campaign at the point of recording the data
- **Sales by Week**: Calculation of current week's cumulative sales minus last week's cumulative sales. (In above screenshot, the calculation is: cell F5 = E5 – E4)
- **Cumulative ROAS**: Calculation of Return on Ad Spend since campaign began. Sales are discounted to reflect true company sales, not Amazon gross sales. For this example, I am calculating ROAS at 75% of Amazon's sales. (In above screenshot, the calculation is: cell G8 = (E8 * .75) / C8)
- **ROAS by Week:** Calculation of Return on Ad Spend by week. Sales are discounted to reflect true company sales, not Amazon gross sales. For this example, I am calculating ROAS at using sales as 75% of Amazon's reported sales. (In above screenshot, the calculation is: cell H8 = (F8 * .75) / D8)

Those are the columns and each week is a different row. I look at AMS data every week, so at the same time each week. I open this sheet so I only pull in only **two numbers** from the dashboard per

110

campaign: *Sales* (Column C above) and *Spend* (Column E). Once I input those in the spreadsheet, I have it set up to automatically subtract the total from last week's total to back into the week's spend. Now I can easily see this week's performance and compare it to prior weeks. If you want to also pull in impressions, clicks, and aCPCs from the AMS dashboard, you can use the same format, just add columns for those data points.

REPORTS

An alternative to the Snapshots method is pulling reports from each campaign, dumping them into a spreadsheet, and then pulling a report from that data. This method cuts out the manual process of looking at the dashboard and recording the numbers. For this method, start at the beginning of your list of campaigns, click into the "Reports" tab and adjust the period you want to look at (such as the previous week) by selecting the dates, then download the report. You can then copy that data and paste it into a spreadsheet you have already set up in order to bring in the totals of each campaign. You would still need to set up calculations to determine each campaign's ROAS.

This method isn't perfect either—when you have dozens of reports, it can take quite a while just to download the reports, much less copying and keeping your spreadsheets straight.

SETTING BUDGETS

I am an advocate for setting a ROAS target and leaving the ads on as long as they are hitting the target. When I say this, I mean looking at the *cumulative* ROAS, not the *weekly* ROAS. Since the attribution window is 14 days, your spend will not always hit during the same week as your sales, and definitely not the same day (if you wanted to analyze by day). That is why I think a "Cumulative ROAS" is an important column to have in your Snapshot sheet or other method, so you can see how the ROAS performs over time. I have had campaigns where I had spending on ads, but ZERO in sales, so $0 ROAS. Then, the next week, I had barely had any spend, and sales that came in later that were attributed to the click on the ad from the previous week. In those cases, you could have weeks where
 ⁻ᵈ $2 and have $800 in sales. Those, of
  ᵗ weeks! However, you know that
  , need to be looked at over a longer
  ʈhat is where the cumulative ROAS

112

comes in—you can see how it is trending. These weekly jumps normalize over time and you can see how the ROAS figure is holding: a bad week won't really tank it and an incredible week won't inflate it too much once your campaign has been running for a while (another reason to keep campaigns on continuously).

KEEP ON RUNNING

My reason for this is: *You never know....* You never know if an external event suddenly may drive a large number of people to Amazon to search for a product like yours. You never know what sales you could scoop up in the off season just by getting your item out there in front of people. You never know the ground you could gain on your competitors by keeping your products in campaigns all year while theirs are not. Now, of course, the huge caveat is that you need to keep the campaigns above your ROAS target. Luckily, I have found this easiest on AMS over other digital ad platforms—but you still need to be able to pinpoint that *true* ROAS.

If you aren't hitting those goals, start testing. Move the levers to see what you happens when you test. This is primarily applicable to the Search and

Display Ads which have the small creative and messaging element that you can test. However, you can also go into Sponsored Products Ads and adjust keywords and bids to hit your goals.

If you are looking at your numbers weekly (or biweekly, as you prefer) and feel comfortable that your ROAS targets are where they should be, then I say don't turn the campaigns off. Just make them work for you all year long. Even if you are keeping bids low and there isn't much traffic, there's no reason to shut the ads off—just keep them running and keep your products in front of the people who are searching for your product!

Appendix A - BONUS:
The Quick-Start Guide to Amazon Advertising

Skip straight to the good stuff and read the details later. Grab your credit card—here we go!

Sponsored Product Ads are the quickest to set up and have great return on ad spend, so start with those.

1. Login with your AMS Vendor ID. Click on the "New Campaign" box in the upper left corner.
2. Choose the "Sponsored Products" selection.
3. Move down to the "Choose Your Products to Advertise" section. For this campaign, choose all your products and create what I call a "Catalog" campaign,

a great one to start with. Select all your products you want to put in the campaign by clicking "Add." The campaign summary on the right will show you what has been selected.

4. Scroll down to "Choose your Campaign" settings. Remember, you can *never change this name*, so choose wisely. Name it something like "Sponsored Catalog Auto Target."

5. Next, you will select Auto or Manual Targeting. Choose Auto; Amazon does the work for you and targets shoppers based on their search terms and matches up your product based on its description. Start with Auto Target and you can move to Manual later, using what you learned.

6. Set your average daily budget. You can select a budget as small as $1 a day. You can change your budget at any time.

7. Set your duration. You have two options: choose a date range or run continuously. Pick "run continuously" since you can pause or terminate the campaigns at any time.

8. Set your cost per click. The CPC will apply to all keywords that Amazon automatically targets. Amazon uses an auction-based pricing model, which

means you will pay $0.01 above the next highest bidder. You can change CPC at any time.

All set! Your ads will be live in less than an hour.

Appendix B - BONUS:
Generate 3 Dozen Keywords in Less Than 10 Minutes

YUM CO KEYWORD EXERCISE

For this example exercise, let's say the holidays are approaching—prime baking season—so Yum Co could start with its cookie cutter category to make sure Headline Search Ads are all up and running and ready for the season. These keywords can also be used in Sponsored Products with manually-selected targeting.

Let's look at the non-brand keywords Yum Co could use.

Here are a few obvious ones:

1. Cookie cutter
2. Cookie
3. Baking cookies
4. Special cookie cutters
5. Baking tools
6. Cookie tools

Now some misspellings and plural/singular form:
7. cooky cutter
8. cokie cutter
9. cooky
10. cookies cutter
11. cookie cutters
12. cookiecutter

TIP: It doesn't cost anything to add keywords and you NEVER know what is going to send people to your products, so just keep adding!

Think about a person's mindset when shopping for your product, or in this case, for cookie cutters:
13. pinterest type cookies
14. fancy cookies
15. birthday party favor cookies
16. party cookies
17. DIY cookies
18. collectible baking tools

19. cookies for kids
20. party favor cookies

Now we'll add a translation:
21. cortador de galletas

Now specific terms that describe Yum Co's line of cookie cutters:
22. girl cookie cutters
23. Easter cookie cutters
24. egg cookie cutters
24. plastic cookie cutter
25. Christmas cookie cutters
26. copper cookie cutters
27. high quality cookie cutters

There are also "long tail" search words you can add, which means a longer phrase that is very specific. Amazon recommends your stick to a few words, but if you want to test, go ahead and add them.
28. cookies for farm birthday party
29. Baking tools for a wedding gift
30. cheap kitchen stuff for a gift

Now we can look at what Amazon suggests for Yum Co. You can find this list when you click "Add Keywords" on the Keywords tab of a campaign. I found the words AMS suggests are somewhat related, but not a word I think people would use to get to my products. Usually the words Amazon suggests belong in another campaign (like a non-brand term when I'm creating a competitive term campaign or a non-brand term for a different product category.), but you can always test!

You can also see what auto-populates when you begin to search for your product. You might be familiar with this from Google (which is where you can also use this trick), but it also works in Amazon. Go the search bar in Amazon and begin to type your keywords. Suggestions will be shown in the drop down box below the search box and below the category suggestions before you click search. I did this for "cookie cutter" and got some great ones:

31. Cookie Cutters for Kids
32. Cookies cutters shapes
33. Cookie cutter set
34. Mini cookie cutters
35. Cookie cutter letters
36. Halloween cookie cutters

Bonus on terms found this way: you know these are terms Amazon customers are *using*.

If you go through this exercise, you should easily have a few dozen or so keywords to start your Headline Search campaign. If you use the "Broad Match" selection, then much of this isn't necessary;

you just need the most basic keywords. However, if you are in a competitive category and don't have the budget to *bid* competitively on common non-brand words in your category, you can scoop up the cheaper exact match phrases using this exercise. The above examples above all fall under a non-brand keyword designation, which will deliver the most volume (in contrast to brand and competitive keywords) and should be created first. After this, Yum Co could create a branded terms campaign and competitor terms campaign as well.

Appendix C – BONUS:
25 Headline Examples to Get Your Campaign Going

Clear writer's block with these 25 headline examples:

1. Dad Will Flip for This Father's Day Gift
2. Stop Your Search! Unique ____ for Your Pet
3. It's Party Time! Shop Unique ____
4. Find the Softest ____ for Fall
5. Pocket-sized ____
6. Measure with Precision & Accuracy
7. Body Scrub that Invigorates
8. Nourish Your Skin with Acme ____
9. 18 Colors of the Longest Lasting ____
10. The Only ____ You'll Ever Need
11. ____ Reinvented
12. Rugged ____ for the Great Outdoors

13. Try Acme ____ Today
14. Discover the National Clean ____
15. Discover the Deliciousness of ____
16. Buy Bulk and Save!
17. Ultra-Sharp ____
18. Shop Lightweight ____
19. Shop Acme Durable
20. Save Now on ____ (this is Proctor & Gamble uses)
21. Keep Your ____ Cool On-the-Go
22. Always be ready! Shop Acme ____
23. Exclusive to Amazon, ____
24. Acme ____ in 10 Styles
25. Buy now, Acme ____ won't last

Appendix D – BONUS:
Campaign Example List by Phase

Here is an example for a fictional business, Driest, that sells umbrellas on Amazon. They have seven ASINs:

1. Driest windproof umbrella-large
2. Driest windproof umbrella-compact
3. Driest travel umbrella
4. Driest golf umbrella
5. Driest value-priced umbrella
6. Driest kids umbrella-blue
7. Driest kids umbrella-orange

The best-selling SKU is the windproof umbrella-compact.

PHASE I

Sponsored Products > Auto Target:

- Campaign: *Full catalog*: windproof umbrella large, windproof umbrella compact, travel umbrella, golf umbrella, value-priced umbrella, kids umbrella blue, kids umbrella orange
- Campaign: *Product assortments or single product*: Kids umbrellas
- Campaign: *Product assortment or single product*: Windproof umbrellas
- Campaign: *Product assortment or single product:* Value umbrella
- Campaign: *Product assortment or single product:* Golf umbrella

PHASE II

- **Sponsored Products > Manual Target (using keyword learning from Auto Target Campaigns)**
  - Campaign: *Product assortment or product:* Kids umbrella blue, Kids umbrella orange
  - Campaign: *Product assortment or single product*: Windproof umbrellas large, windproof umbrella compact

128

- o Campaign: *Product assortment or single product:* Value umbrella
- o Campaign: *Product assortment or single product:* Golf umbrella
- **Headline Search Ads**
  - o Campaign: *Brand:* Driest
    - Keywords include: Driest, Driest umbrellas, Driest brand kids umbrellas
  - o Campaign: *Non Brand*: Featuring Windproof compact, landing page includes all SKUs (can repeat for the rest of the SKUs)
  - o Campaign: *Competitive*: Featuring Windproof compact, landing page includes all SKUs
    - Keywords include: Totes umbrellas, Kolumbo umbrella
  - o Campaign: *Non Brand*: Kids, landing page features kids SKUs, plus compact & value SKUs
    - Keywords include: kids umbrellas, umbrellas for toddlers, children's umbrellas
- **Product Display Ads > Target by Product (can do one of these for all seven)**

- o Campaign: *Complementary products*: Rain boots
  - o Campaign: *Complementary products*: Raincoats

PHASE III

- Product Display Ads > Target by Product
  - o Campaign: Competitors
    - Target Totes SKUs
- Product Display Ads > Target by Interest
  - o Campaign: *Interest*: Luggage

Campaign Example List by Phase: Company with full line of products

PHASE I

- Sponsored Products
  - o Auto Target
    - Full catalog
    - Product assortments or single product

PHASE II

- Sponsored Products
  - o Manual Target

- By product assortment or product
- Headline Search Ads
  - Brand
  - Non brand (for each category)
  - Competitor (for each category)
- Product Display Ads
  - Target by Product (could be for each product, or just top sellers)
    - Complementary products

PHASE III

- Product Display Ads
  - Target by Product (could be for each product, or just top sellers)
    - Competitors
  - Target by interest

Thank you!

If you have enjoyed this book or found it helpful,
I'd like to ask a favor: would you mind reviewing it
on Amazon.com? It would be greatly appreciated!

Acknowledgements

I'd like to thank my editor Tamara VanWormer for
her thorough polishing of my rough manuscript and
Daniel Willis for his beautiful formatting.

Made in the USA
Middletown, DE
20 June 2020